'They're Only A Breath Away'

The Remarkable True Story of Medium Christina Green

Published By Christina Green.

C Green has asserted her right under the Copyright,
Designs and Patents Act 1988, to be identified as the author of this work.

All photographs are under copyright to the author.

Printed in Great Britain by Cox and Wyman Ltd, Reading.

'They're only a breath away' can be ordered via e-mail
guardianwhitea@aol.co.uk
and for future appearances and demonstrations see
http://christinagreenclairvoyant.webs.com

ISBN 978-0-9566485-0-1

I dedicate this book to my sister Lou (Linda)

'In my beginning is my end... and in my end, is my beginning.'

T.S. Eliot

Thanks to John Parker, my ghostwriter,
for your help in writing this book

One

Where does the story of a person's life begin? Since we usually start with the time and place of birth, I'll begin by telling you that I was born in south London, in East Dulwich Hospital to be precise, in 1957. There was a new Prime Minister that year, Harold McMillan, Cliff Richard was just seventeen, and about to become an overnight star as the Rock and Roll craze swept Britain. The average weekly wage was £14 before tax, which doesn't sound a lot, but then again a pint of beer was little more than a shilling, or 5 pence - and you could buy your own house for under £2,000.

This then was the world I was born into. But just as our lives move forward and take shape after our birth, so, for each one of us, there is a part of our story that has already been written, a part we have not witnessed. These mysterious, hidden chapters, often rich with drama and emotion, lived out before we were even a twinkle in someone's eye, may reveal much about our own early experiences, the nature of our family relationships, and how we as children are regarded, things which can otherwise seem baffling.

So what are the 'hidden chapters' that lie behind my own story? To view them we must travel further back in time, to some fifteen years before my arrival. The scene opens in the dark days of the war, an era of hardship and danger for so many people, and foreshadowing a series of events, which, for my family, were destined to bring a particular kind of heartache.

By 1941, Londoners like my mum and dad had already experienced life at the sharp end, by way of the Blitz. Thousands of civilians - men, women and children – were to perish in the air raids, and the nightly wail of the sirens, followed by the dreaded doodle-bugs and other fiendish devices which dropped from the sky, were still bringing fear and destruction to cities all over Britain.

Amidst the horror and death, ordinary life still went on of course, including the other fundamental aspects of human existence, marriage, lovemaking and birth. My mother, at this time in her early twenties had already had one child, a little girl. Now she wanted an addition, and not just any child; she had set her heart on a boy. When she next fell pregnant, her hopes were high. The child, born prematurely, turned out however to be another girl. Though Mother was disappointed, my father was delighted, welcoming his newborn daughter as a precious gift. As the days went by Dad watched over her tiny, frail body, willing it to grow, strengthen, and return his loving smiles. At just six weeks old however, the little one died.

Dad was devastated. My mother by all accounts was far more matter of fact, the loss only intensifying her longing for a boy. A short while later she was pregnant again. Once more she hoped, and once more was disappointed with another girl. Arriving more or less on time, little Peggy as they named her, was a healthier offspring. My father was again thrilled, and as the weeks passed he at least must have been relieved to see his new daughter putting on some weight. His happiness was once again to be shattered however, when, at six months old, Peggy succumbed to what we now know as cot death. My mother, who had shown little enthusiasm for Peggy's birth, was equally unmoved by her dying.

My father at this time was busy supporting the family, working as a window-cleaner in Crystal Palace and the surrounding area. It seemed he was home some of the time, since my mother soon became pregnant again. This time, she thought, the law of averages must surely be on her side and bless her with a male offspring. Confident of the fact, she continued to go out and about despite the air raids, looking forward to the birth of what she felt sure would be her long hoped for son. Her predictions were correct in one sense. The Luftwaffe pilots however were not choosy where they dropped their payloads, and one night a stray bomb fell near the local cinema. My mother happened to be inside. The collateral damage brought down some masonry, and she suffered slight injuries. Though not seriously hurt, the shock had been enough to affect the child she was carrying, which a few weeks later, was stillborn. My mother's distress lay chiefly in the fact that it was indeed, a boy.

Though already dead, the child required a burial, and therefore a name, and Robert was decided on. How he must have haunted my mother's dreams. Did she I wonder, torture herself over going out to the cinema that fateful night, placing the guilt on herself?

Meanwhile, despite, or perhaps because of what had happened, she resolved to try again. Possibly now knowing she could produce a boy strengthened her resolve. In 1942 she succeeded, with the birth of Michael. I can imagine her joy, and no doubt my father's that at last his wife's deepest need had been gratified. After losing two infants, there must also have been much anxiety over the newborn. Michael however continued growing, and when six months had passed, everyone no doubt breathed a sigh of relief, looking forward to his first birthday.

If there was such optimism, it was to prove misplaced. In those days there was no central heating in most ordinary dwellings. Homes were equipped only with basic coal fires, which in cold weather were hardly adequate to ensure good health, especially for the elderly and young children. Pneumonia was not uncommon, and often fatal, as, at ten months old, it was for little Michael. Mum was inconsolable. Michael's death, after experiencing such happiness, must have felt especially cruel for both parents. The grief this time cut Mum like a knife. For almost a year she had cuddled her little boy and watched him smile, comforted him when he cried, felt his tiny hand curl around her fingers. The bond between mother and son had grown through love, and become complete. Then without rhyme or reason he had been snatched away from her forever.

As with any fatal illness or accident, particularly involving a child, my parents were not only emotionally wounded by this tragedy, but must also have felt a sense of deep injustice. Both were members of the Church of England, and though only attending services on special occasions, believed in the Christian message of love and eternal life. Christianity also teaches that all things happen for a reason. After Michael died, the question of 'why?' hung particularly heavily in my father's thoughts. What divine purpose could there be here? If there was a loving Father watching over us from heaven, why had he inflicted such distress?

The loss of the previous children had been endured stoically; the Bible teaches that God works in mysterious ways, and that our faith in him will often be tested. Michael though had been almost one year old, a little person, so long awaited and so full of promise, promise for the future, of a life here on earth with a family. 'Blessed are the mournful,' Jesus said, 'for they will be comforted.' For my father, another Biblical quote was sounding more appropriate: the last straw breaks the camel's back. For him Michael's death was a test too far, and at this point in his life he made it plain he no longer believed in God.

As for my mother, she had buried Robert, the boy who had never lived, only to face the ordeal of burying a son who had had a life. With both children, she may also have attempted to bury emotions too extreme to deal with. Whether or not she managed to stifle her feelings, they were destined to surface later, and to have dire consequences for those around her, myself included.

Meanwhile, Michael's demise was to be far from the last of the couple's trials. Just as the war was coming to an end, Mum gave birth to a little girl, Gloria. At six months old she too was gone, another victim of unexplained cot death. It would have been understandable if my parents had decided enough was enough at this point, and been content to settle down as a family of three with my older sister. Maybe they did call it a day, for a while at least. What was it that later on changed their minds?

Possibly it had something to do with a dramatic event, which, in 1952, seven years after the war ended, and little Gloria's death, was to turn their whole world upside down. It began as just another ordinary working day for my dad, who, now employed as a lorry driver, was delivering a load of timber to a building under construction. While carrying the wood up some scaffolding, one of the boards beneath him gave way. It was nearly a fifty-foot drop to the ground.

When Dad hit the bottom, no one could have expected him to survive. At the hospital the doctors found almost every bone in his body was broken, and by the time they had finished, nearly every part of him was encased in plaster. It wasn't only his bones that were damaged. When he finally regained consciousness, it was discovered that my father was unable to see.

Two

As the days turned into weeks, dad's broken bones slowly healed. The relief that he had survived his incredible fall and was recovering, was now marred by a growing concern for his eyesight, which showed no sign of improvement. The prognosis was not good, all the indications being that he would henceforth be permanently blind.

As soon as his injuries would allow, he was brought home, where he now had to be helped much of the time. Most forms of work being closed to him, in order to learn how to cope he was enrolled in a college for the blind. For a man who had been so active and used to the freedom of the open road, it must have been very difficult for my poor dad to come to terms with this new and bewildering situation. My mother and older sister were also affected, not least by the financial consequences of losing a breadwinner.

For the next two years the family struggled, shuffling between the college, to visit my dad, and trying to make ends meet at home. Then one day, something remarkable happened. My father began to report misty shapes appearing behind his eyes. The doctors were summoned, and various tests run. As the days went by the misty shapes hardened, and my father was able to make out outlines, see chairs and tables close to him. Before long he could recognise faces, including those of his wife and daughter. The improvements in his vision continued, until very soon his eyesight was fully restored, and he was able to leave the college and return home.

From all the fractures he had sustained, my father still had aches and pains, as well as a pronounced limp, which looked set to remain with him. Another permanent disfigurement was to his face, one side of which remained paralysed. To everyone's amazement however, he soon returned to his former employment as a lorry driver. His friends and workmates, welcoming him back, from now on hailed him as 'The Miracle Man'. It must indeed have seemed a miracle, like something out of the Bible. If my mum had given prayers, it seemed they had been well and truly answered.

If thanking God, she may also have thought about the significance of what had happened, and why. My father had not only been spared death at the moment of the dreadful accident, now his sight had been given back. Both he and my mother seemed to have been given some kind of second chance. Was it this reprieve, which, after so long spurred thoughts of having a son again? My mother had already been advised that given her history, further attempts at childbirth would be unwise.

She was not however one to listen to medical opinion, or anyone else's, when it came to this. About two years after my father's recovery, she began feeling ill one day, and was sent for tests. Since she was now forty-one, she was told it was most likely the onset of her menopause. She thought otherwise, and was convinced she was pregnant. The doctors took some x-rays, ruling out pregnancy, but my mother stuck to her assertion and requested further investigation. Six months later, on the sixth x-ray, something was revealed. Pressed up close against Mum's spine was a tiny shape. The shape grew larger, and it was confirmed; she was indeed carrying a child.

Naturally she thought of a boy. The 'second chance' from God, after the long ordeal of one dead child after another, might now be about to fulfil its grand design – and to heal the aching wound left by the loss of little Michael. As the time drew close, everything was prepared, and while my mother went into hospital to await the birth, my father set about busily painting the house. When the phone rang on the due day, he put down his paintbrush and hurried to pick up the receiver. Sure enough it was the maternity ward, to say the baby had arrived. Thanking the nurse, he hung up and turned to my older sister. 'It's a girl,' he said, then added, 'Mum's not going to be pleased.'

Thankfully I emerged healthy, to begin with at least. Dad, no doubt remembering poor Michael, was very concerned to protect me from any possible ailments, keeping me warm and safe at all times, wrapping me in cotton wool as the saying goes. Mum on the other hand, preferred that I should be out in the garden whenever possible, subscribing to the 'plenty of fresh air does them good' school of thought.

Perhaps between them they achieved a happy medium, as I reached the age of ten months without complication. Ten months became eleven, then the magical one year old. My first birthday must have been a bit of a red-letter day in the household, being only the second of my parent's otherwise ill-fated children to survive as long.

Two months later my mother gave birth again, though alas for her, not to a boy. This must have been a touch and go affair too, since the baby arrived very premature. This made me an in-between of a slightly unusual kind, having a big sister twenty years my senior, and with me, and my baby sister, Linda, just fourteen months apart.

It was shortly after Linda's arrival, a good half way towards my second birthday that things started to go wrong for me. Taken ill, and never one to do things by halves, I was diagnosed with double pneumonia and taken into hospital. As my father sat hour after hour at my bedside, hoping and praying despite his disillusionment with God, that he wasn't about to lose yet another child, I lay there lingering. To try to keep both our spirits up he would lean over and sing me a song called 'Tammy', which had been a hit for Debbie Reynolds.

One day at the hospital there came terror for my dad. Quite suddenly I was seized by a cardiac arrest. Acting swiftly, the medical staff managed to resuscitate me. A short while later it happened again, and again the nurses were able to bring me back. Then came a third attack, and this time the situation was very different. The first nurse to rush to my side was unable to restore my breathing or find a pulse, and urgently summoned assistance. In an instant her colleagues were surrounding the bed, and it was all hands to the pump in a desperate bid to restart my heart and induce vital signs. After several minutes of feverish activity on my inert body, the senior doctor made a grim pronouncement: there was nothing more they could do. My father, who might have been expected at this point to collapse with grief, simply refused to accept what he had been told. Frantically he urged the doctors to continue, to please, please, please save his child. Persuaded by him, they resumed their efforts. Within a few minutes I began breathing again.

Whether any of the doctors or nurses actually believed there was hope for me at that crucial moment, or whether they were placating a distraught father, I will never know. What I do know is that I died that day in hospital, and that it was effectively my dad who brought me back to life. But something had happened to me in the process, the returned child was different. Before the illness, like most eighteen month olds, I had started walking and talking. Now it was found I could do neither, a reversal in my development that must have been worrying. Slowly but surely, I learned to balance and move my limbs once more, toddle around the room, and to form words again.

Following this 'death' or near-death experience, a momentary crossing over, call it what you will, another change had taken place. It was something that couldn't yet be observed, but which would soon manifest itself in my thoughts, and, much to my parents' concern, my behaviour. I must have been about two years old when I first woke in the middle of the night to see someone in my room. There was no one actually there, or rather, no one in the earthly sense. This was unlike anyone I had ever seen in my everyday world. Stood silently at the end of my bed, the figure was dressed in long flowing robes of blue and white, and on their head wore a strange looking square hat. My first impression was of an angel, like those I had seen in religious pictures and Bible illustrations. I felt afraid, but also curious.

When the figure appeared again I thought she was more like a nun. I began to tell my big sister about these visitations. 'My nun was here again last night' I would say. My sister would tell me I had just been dreaming, that was all. Sometimes the visitations would really scare me, and I would cry out in the night. My parents would then tell me to go back to bed - it was only a dream, only a dream. If my sister woke she might sometimes come in and talk to me. 'Did your nun come again?' she would ask, then add, half serious half amused, 'I don't suppose she knows where my blinking shoes are, I can't find them anywhere!'

The nun was not my only visitor. One night I woke in amazement to see above my bed, a troupe of dancers in colourful costumes. They were waltzing, swirling, moving gracefully in time, round and round before my eyes, as if in some glamorous ballroom hung with chandeliers, or on a great stage. As each passed by, they would turn their lovely smiling faces towards me. They appeared to be half disembodied, having no legs, floating in the air with their long, silky robes flowing almost transparent around them. They never spoke to me, or to each other. They seemed happy simply to be dancing, carried blissfully along to the strains of an invisible orchestra, giving themselves up to the sheer joy of movement, lost in the moment.

My dancers were an enchanting sight, and whenever they put on their little nocturnal show for me I would always feel comforted, and drift peacefully off to sleep.

Three

Along with my silent, hovering nun and the lovely dancers, other odd things were going on in my head. Not all of them were pleasant. Day or night, for no apparent reason I would often feel afraid or upset and start crying. The crying would go on and on, trying my mother's patience. This, along with my continuing urge to tell everyone about my visions, were I suppose, what unleashed certain unforgettable repercussions.

My big sister, by this time a grown up woman in her early twenties, listened to the things I told her with an airy indulgence, treating me in fact as the small child I was. Initially my mother also indulged my tales of funny people floating over my bed, though never considered they might be anything other than dreams, Before long though she began to find the night time waking and the weird stories, and particularly the crying, to be irksome. Very soon she regarded the whole situation as downright disturbing. Now she got angry when I woke her up or told her about the nun and the dancers. On bad days she would tell me I was evil. As she got increasingly cross, I likewise became more upset.

Things quickly went from bad to worse. My emotions seemed to boil over on occasion, and, in a torrent of frustration and fear my body would frequently be wracked with convulsions, and on occasion, epileptic fits. These fits, which could occur day or night, were naturally very concerning to my mother, and in desperation she called on the doctor for advice. Between them, it was decided the best way to calm me down at such times was to confine me alone in a room. Thus it was, when I next broke out into one of my fits, my mother marched me to a cupboard in the wall, thrust me inside and closed the door. It was horrible to be shut in, and made me shout and scream even more. Only when I had made myself too weak to cry any more did mother release me, exhausted and whimpering.

Worse though was to follow. Our house, an old, and to me cavernous Victorian dwelling, with many dark, unexplored recesses, had at the very bottom what was called 'the downstairs room'. This room, though not quite a cellar, was semi subterranean, and part of what had formerly been a ground floor flat, for a long time empty. When the time came for my older sister to marry, she and her husband moved into this flat, where they soon had children of their own. They did not however use the very lowest part of the house, the downstairs room, which remained mysteriously out of bounds. Missing my sister, and to get away from my mother's indifference or wrath, I got into the habit of wandering down to the flat in search of more sympathetic company. For some reason this really angered my mother, who, if she noticed my absence would come thundering down to find me, screaming that if I wanted to live with my sister she would move my bed down there.

One day during one of my emotional outbursts, rather than taking me to the cupboard as usual, my mother took me down to the flat. But she didn't stop there. Instead she opened the door to the stairs that led to the very deepest part of the house, the disused 'downstairs room'. Bustling me inside, she then departed without a word and I was left alone.

I stood in shock, quivering in the brooding space, blinking in the half-light, too fearful to move, terrified of what might be lurking in the dark interior that lay beyond. The room was silent, with sinister looking shapes, and shrouded objects that seemed to rise up out of the shadows. In every visible nook and cranny cobwebs hung in clumps, heavy with dust, or in wispy, trailing strands. Groping for something solid to hold on to, I nervously reached out and touched one of the shapes, which immediately coated my hand in thick dust, making me recoil.

On the far side of the room, from a grimy low-level window, a narrow shaft of daylight filtered in, partially illuminating an old wooden rocking chair. I wanted to move towards the window and reach the light, but as I approached something made me stop and turn my face away. Something about the chair made me afraid. It was the only item of furniture not covered over, but unlike everything else in the room, there was no dust on it. When I looked again it seemed to be moving, swaying back and forth, creaking very softly, as if some invisible person was sitting there waiting for me, for some terrible reason I could not understand, perhaps to punish me again.

Trying once more to steady myself, I rested my fingertips gingerly on another of the lumpy shapes. As I did so something slid beneath my touch, a sheet, which slid to the floor. Underneath was a small table.

On touching it I felt something skitter over my skin. I screamed and ran back, shaking my arm violently, while a huge black spider scuttled across the floor and disappeared in a dark corner. I shrieked again, and ran towards the door, hammering on it with my small hands, shouting and crying to be let out.

Four

My mother had obviously locked me in the downstairs room for a reason. Maybe it was spite at my preferring my big sister's company. More likely she had had enough of my crying in the cupboard. Hidden several floors below, I was out of earshot. How long I kicked and hammered and bawled to be let out I do not know. It seemed like hours, but perhaps it was only minutes. The sense of relief, when eventually I heard my mother's footsteps coming, is all I can be sure of.

It wasn't the last time I was confined there. Fear of the place, which was intense, didn't stop my fits since these were involuntary and beyond my control. Sometimes I was put there simply for talking about my visions, which increasingly seemed to touch a nerve with my mother. It was something she could neither understand nor control, and when I told her about seeing people in my room, or of any dream that seemed unusual, she would order me to stop such thoughts and repeat her accusation - that I was evil.

Probably she believed this. Being a religious woman, the idea of the devil, and the fear of going to hell might have been very real. From early on I can remember her instructing my sister and I in prayers, 'Our Father, who art in heaven, forgive us our trespasses… and deliver us from evil…' I even had my own little altar, housed in a cupboard, with a cross and a picture of Jesus to which I would kneel and pray each night.

Generally I remained a nervous and sickly child, but at least, after the age of about three the epileptic fits subsided. Like most children then, I was five years old before I started my education. My older sister would take me to school, walking down the hill to Rockmount Juniors in West Norwood. What I loved most was painting. One day the headmistress took me into her office and said she was going to put one of my pictures on her wall. I remember feeling very pleased and proud about this.

Fitting in I found hard. I dearly wanted to make friends, but all my attempts seemed awkward and unsuccessful. As a result I spent a lot of time on my own, and once regarded as a loner, the pattern became set. At school lunchtime, I rarely had an appetite, which was thought

17

curable by having a teacher stand behind me urging me to eat. I began to get very bad headaches, and though I told the teachers, I was usually thought to be faking it to get out of lessons. As a result of the enforced eating, when I got home I would often be violently sick. I was probably experiencing migraines, at that time not much known about.

. It wasn't long before my younger sister had joined me at Rockmount. Linda and I had already displayed marked differences in our personalities, and these became much more apparent in school. She seemed to join in naturally, and was always off somewhere with her friends at playtime, while I would be sat on a bench. Despite chalk and cheese natures, Linda and I were extremely close. I had always felt very protective of her, and whenever she was sick or fractious I would nurse to her. At night in our shared room I would cuddle her in bed till she went off to sleep, like she was my baby. In fact she was a good sleeper, and once off there was little that could wake her. I was the one who slept lightly, especially when my 'visitors' were with me.

Our mother's attitude to both Linda and I was cold and remote, in that we were never cuddled by her, and she would push us away. But though she withheld affection equally, she was partial with her blame, and with any misdemeanour, whoever had been at fault she tended to scold only me. Even when I knew this to be unfair I held my tongue, not through virtue, but the desire to shield Linda from any kind of harm or distress.

As we played and grew together, Linda began to emerge more and more as the high-spirited one, with an irrepressible, often spitfire temperament about her. As these traits sharpened, Mum's attitude towards the two of us diverged further, and she treated us quite differently. As time went on I found myself being physically separated from Linda on occasions, notably during the summer holidays, when she would be taken off to stay with relatives on Mum's side of the family out in Oxfordshire, while I was left at home. I was never entirely sure why this was. Perhaps, being a child who was quiet in company, it was felt I wouldn't fit in with the group. Possibly though it was reactive behaviour on my mother's part; within the family I was 'Daddy's girl', and staking a claim on Linda could have been Mum's way of emotionally playing him off. Perhaps too, in Linda's tough and feisty nature, my mother saw the son she had always longed for. Whatever distances might be placed between us however, the bond connecting Linda and I was unbreakable. In time she got to know about my spirit visitors, and would ask me what things my 'angel' had said.

There was a similar, perfect bond of love between my dad and I. Knowing that he enjoyed going to football matches, on my sixth birthday, when he asked me what I would like, I said I wanted to 'see the football' with him. The fact I didn't ask for dolls or a tea set may have come as a surprise, but Dad seemed delighted nonetheless, and as a fan of our local side Crystal Palace, he proudly took me along to their next game.

The companionship between Dad and I, our enjoyment of simple things and just being together, grew stronger. When I was old enough, during the school holidays he would take me with him in his lorry on trips. There was a great sense of adventure, stopping off at transport cafes for lunch then back on route, seeing the fields and hedges flash by as we headed out into the countryside. On long journeys we would pull into a lay-by and stay overnight, Dad, bless him, stretching out in the cab so I could have the special driver's bunk bed overhead.

On these excursions I was not the 'quiet' girl of home, but in his words 'never stopped talking', which he loved. Dad meanwhile would sing the Beatles' songs to me as he drove. We travelled near and far, seeing the beautiful plants and scenery of Devon, and even down into Wales on occasion, just my lovely dad and me, together on the open road. These were wonderful days, and I never, ever wanted them to end.

Five

By the mid 1960s increasing numbers of families in Britain were acquiring a television set. It must have been towards the end of 1964 that my mother announced we too would be getting a TV for my birthday.

Coming up to eight years old, I thought this a fantastic present. When the set arrived however, it was placed in the 'special' room of the house, reserved for when my dad was home, or visitors. At all other times it was kept locked, and my sister Linda and I were not allowed in. My eagerly awaited 'present' remained out of sight, and out of bounds.

One night the phone rang. My mother had been expecting the call, as it was my dad, on his way back from a long distance trip to say what time he would be home. When he arrived I immediately went to him, and told him about something I had seen. 'What was it?' he asked. I said that I had seen a funeral, of Sir Winston Churchill. Dad said this was impossible, since it had not yet taken place. But I had seen it I insisted, and described the scene - the service at Westminster Abbey, the crowds of mourners, and the coffin being carried by barge along the river Thames towards the great man's resting place at his family home of Blenheim Palace.

The next morning the special room was unlocked, the television switched on, and my dad and I sat down together and watched the funeral of Sir Winston Churchill. The whole event, broadcast live, was just as I had described it. Dad was certainly surprised and asked Mum how I could have known so much detail before it happened.. I can't remember Mum's reply - I simply told Dad I had seen it all in a dream, which was true.

Getting a television wasn't the only milestone for our family in 1965. A far bigger change was in store. One day a man from the council called round and told my parents that the houses on either side of us were to be demolished. 'What of it?' they asked. He explained that since this would make our property unsound, it was best if ours came down too.

Having lived there for years, my mum and dad were naturally taken aback and wanted to know more - in particular, where they were supposed to go. The man told them a new estate would be built on the site, and while it was under construction they would be provided with temporary accommodation. When the work was finished, one of the brand new houses would be theirs to live in, complete with lots of wonderful, up to date fittings and fixtures. All in all, they would end up much better off.

No doubt my parents thought hard about this sudden, out of the blue decision they were being asked to make, not without misgivings. The big Central Hill property had its drawbacks, particularly in the winter with draughty windows and inadequate heating. On the other hand, moving was a big upheaval, and was it really necessary? Supposing they defied the council's recommendations and refused to go? They were assured the move was not merely advisable, but essential for safety reasons. Our house though was detached, so the demolition of neighbouring properties surely wouldn't affect it. Were they being told the truth they wondered, and if not, what should they do about it?

While the future of our house hung in the balance, I became quite unwell one day, running a high temperature. Mum kept dosing me up with aspirin, but things got worse. Finally, a couple of days short of my ninth birthday, finding I couldn't stand up I was taken into hospital and placed in an isolation room. It was suspected I had polio. When the diagnosis arrived it turned out to be aspirin poisoning.

On the home front, decisions were soon taken out of our hands. Lambeth council issued a compulsory purchase order on the whole street, notices to quit were served, and a moving date set. My parents, though sad at the prospect of leaving the family home, which held so many memories for them, did their best to think of the future. At least they would remain amongst their friends and neighbours and the area of Upper Norwood and Crystal Palace they were familiar with. All the other families affected by the demolition had been offered places in the new estate once it was built, so we were all in the same boat. Putting a brave face on, Mum and Dad began packing their possessions and looking forward to the new house, with all its promised modern conveniences.

In the meantime we had to move. The halfway house allocated by the council was in Dunbar Place, West Norwood. It couldn't be described as luxury accommodation. We found ourselves in what was known as a prefab, one of a number of small, single storey dwellings, originally erected as makeshift houses for those made homeless by the blitz. These structures, many built by German and Italian prisoners of war, had been intended to last a maximum of ten years. Now, almost a quarter of a century later, we were being dumped here courtesy not of Hitler but Lambeth Council.

Mum and Dad were not at all pleased about the prefab, which, after our rambling house felt cramped and uncomfortable. That year, as the solid brickwork of the fine Victorian houses in Central Hill were reduced to rubble, the families they had been home to sat incarcerated in what were little more than wood and concrete boxes. All we could hope was that it wouldn't be for too long.

Six

The prefab did at least have a garden. While Mum stomped around and complained of 'living in a rabbit hutch', Dad looked at ways to make best use of the outdoor space. One of the first things he did was build Linda and I a wooden swing, which when the weather allowed gave us something to play on, and got us out from under Mum's feet for a bit. The frame of the swing wasn't cemented into the ground, so as we swung the whole thing would move around.

Dad loved the garden, and down the side of the prefab he set to work cultivating a vegetable patch. The crops he grew helped the household finances, since money was tight, and like many other families we had to pull together. Dad worked long shifts as a lorry driver for 'Britain's Joinery' in West Norwood, but by no means earned a fortune, and Mum also had a full time job. After school, being first to arrive home Linda and I would do the housework together, and on Sundays help Mum with the dinner, preparing the vegetables and taking turns with custard or pudding. Since Mum relied on her job, it meant that if Linda were sick, I would stay home and look after her.

School now was St Luke's in West Norwood, to which Linda and I walked two miles each morning, the same coming home. Though I remained a lonely child, I did take part in two plays here, one a Christmas pantomime, in which I played a little Dutch girl, the other a story about life in wartime England. Being C of E, daily prayers were said at our desks first thing in the morning, then again at home time.

With a God-fearing Christian ethos, certain things at St Luke's were deeply frowned upon. While sat in class I would occasionally receive spirit messages about other children, which I would pass on, sometimes going into what they called a trance. Once when this happened, I realised the teacher had been shouting at me for some time. I still could not speak however, which made him even angrier. In front of the class he said what I had done was 'black magic.' This made me cry. I knew what had happened to me wasn't wrong, yet at the same time I felt ashamed.

As the months passed in the confines of the prefab, we settled into some sort of routine, though hardly a cheerful one. Mum's mood was downbeat a lot of the time, and she seemed cross with both Linda and I for no particular reason. She would make comments about wanting to put us both in a home. Whether this was just her tiredness and nerves speaking, or whether she would seriously prefer to get rid of us, we had no way of being sure. Sometimes in a temper she would round on me, saying 'I never wanted you in the first place.'

Not everything was doom and gloom. Through hard work and thrift, we could just about afford to own a family car. It was a Hillman Imp, a popular model then, with the number plate MJD 521, the M and D, as I always thought, standing for Mum and Dad. Linda and I loved the car, and nicknamed her Daisy. She was a saving grace. In summer, we'd all pile into Daisy and Dad would drive us away from the prefab and out of London, to Leysdown, on the Isle of Sheppey, to stay for a few days in a little holiday chalet, complete with amusements, entertainment, and most important of all, the beach.

The moment of arrival, when the sea came into view, bright and sparkling in the distance was always so exciting. The days of fresh air and sunshine that followed were blissful. Dad, always the first one up, would make Mum some tea, and after a piece of toast each, he and I would take a walk along the beach. Mum usually prepared the main meals in the chalet, helped by Linda and I, or if she had one of her headaches, Dad would take over.

Dad loved the old penny in the slot machines, saving his coppers throughout the year to share out with Linda and I. In the evenings, he liked taking us all to the clubhouse, and though a smoker, drank nothing stronger than bitter shandy. It was all he needed - always the life and soul, he would sing along to the Beatles', do the jive and teach Linda and I the twist. Mum preferred to sit back and relax, unless a slow number came on when she might get up for a dance with Dad. Happy, carefree times indeed.

Linda and I were always very sad when the holidays came to an end. It meant back to school, and of course, life in the dreary prefab. One year became two, and there still seemed no news about the estate, or of when we might move into our new house. Central Hill was fast becoming a distant fond memory, with no clear picture of the future to take its place.

Not all had been left behind in our old home. My nocturnal 'visitors' had followed me, and would regularly appear in my bedroom, sometimes murmuring, sometimes content to hover nearby. My nun began to make regular appearances too, and often I would sit fully awake on my bed, just looking at her in her beautiful robes.

One night as I was watching my nun, she suddenly spoke to me. Her voice clear and distinct, she said she had something to tell me, about my father. He was going away, on a long journey. 'Where?' I asked her, then, 'Why?

She said no more, and was gone. I lay down, wondering what it meant. I knew my dad went on journeys because he was a long-distance lorry driver. Why bother telling me? Could there be anything so different about this trip that my nun seemed to think he would be taking. Perhaps it was going to be an especially long one. But however long a time Dad was away for, I knew he always came back. Then I had a sudden panic. Supposing he was planning to leave home and never return! But why on earth would he do that? Even if he wanted to get away from Mum, surely he wouldn't leave me, not ever. But the idea of it made me burst into tears, and I lay there on the bed, violently sobbing, crying my heart out at the thought of being separated from my lovely dad.

After a while there came footsteps. The bedroom door opened and there was Dad, woken by the sound of my crying. He came over and put his arm around me. Whatever was the matter, he asked, had I had a bad dream? 'Why are you going away?' I asked him, tears still streaming down my face. 'What do you mean?' he replied. 'My nun, she said you were going away, on a long journey' I said. Dad smiled kindly and said, 'You were just dreaming, I'm not going anywhere.' Still anxious, I nestled against him and begged again, 'Please don't leave.' 'Shush,' he said softly, 'I'll never leave.'

Maybe, going back to bed my dad smiled to himself about my 'dream' of him going away. Being a lorry driver, it was a bit like the old joke in which the fortune-teller, visited by a sailor in uniform predicts he's going to make a journey over water. My dad hadn't dismissed

25

me though, that wasn't his way. His only concern was to take away my anxiety. That night, just hearing his kind voice and words of reassurance, I slept soundly, in perfect knowledge of his love.

Seven

Things did not end there however. A few nights later, my nun came again, and I was filled with a sense of foreboding. Watching her from the bed, I told myself that perhaps she had come with good news now, to say that my father was not 'going away' after all. When she began speaking I realised that this was not the case. Yes, she said, he was indeed going away. I implored her to tell me more – did she know where or how long he would be gone? All she would say was that I should prepare myself for what was to happen, that I should be ready. Then she was gone. There followed several more visitations, each time with a repetition of the warning, and of the need for readiness and to understand the events that were soon to unfold.

It was not until the March of 1969, that anyone apart from me received the first real hint of what might be to come. It was very early spring, and with the first bright yellow daffodils already flowered and almost gone, it was the time of year when our thoughts usually turned to the warmer days ahead, and soon, our holidays by the sea. Dad, who had been feeling a bit under the weather though, had recently gone to the doctor. The doctor, after giving him an initial check-up, had then sent him for further tests.

Otherwise things seemed normal, and life went on as before. Apart that is, from some news the family had recently received, on a quite different matter. My older sister, who was now living with her husband and children in a house out in New Addington, had learned that some neighbours of theirs were keen to move, and in particular to come further in to south London. The New Addington estate was still quite new; all proper houses with modern features, the sort of place we had been looking forward to on the site of our old home in Central Hill. After almost four years in the prefab however, we had pretty much given up hope on that front. My sister mentioned our situation to her neighbours, and that we were looking for somewhere with more space, and asked if they would be interested in an exchange to West Norwood. The only possible snag was whether the idea of living in a prefab would put them off. It turned out not; they were simply looking to be closer to town, which meant that if everything worked out we could have a smart new spacious home, in the leafy suburbs. An agreement was soon reached, and a date for the exchange set.

Not long before the day of the move we went down to Leysdown for a short break. The weather was bracing, but it was as lovely as ever to be in our favourite place by the sea. It was also only a few weeks till my twelfth birthday. Strolling along the promenade with Dad, Linda and I saw something else we really liked, the roundabout with the big teacups and saucers. Dad knew we couldn't resist, and nodded for us to jump up. We took our seats, Dad paid the fairground man, the machinery whirred, and we started to move.

There was something about this ride that just made you smile. The brightly coloured teacups, some decorated in bold candy stripes, some with huge polka dots, were like a scene out of Alice in Wonderland. As the roundabout picked up speed, the whirling motion and the wind in their hair soon had everyone grinning. Every now and then the fairground man would give each teacup a little twist, sending it spinning wildly round, and setting the occupants off into peals of hysterical laughter. As we circled we waved at Dad as we sped by each time, just catching his returning wave and bright smile before the gyrating cup flicked us away, and round we went again. All too soon the ride began to slow, the teacups stopped spinning and we came to a gentle stop. Linda and I hopped off, and, still giddy and giggling, went to rejoin Dad.

Everything still seemed to be going round before our eyes, and it was hard to stand up, which was quite normal after riding the teacups. As I looked at Dad he appeared to be swaying too. He also seemed to be smiling in a rather strange way, like he was deliberately making a funny face. By the time my balance had returned to normal however, something told me he wasn't joking around. The next minute he seemed to be falling. Linda and I rushed towards him, but he was flat out on the ground. Frantic, we ran into one of the nearby shops, saying our dad was ill and needed help. The shopkeeper straightaway telephoned for an ambulance, and Dad was rushed to hospital, where he was given an emergency operation.

When we went to the hospital to see Dad, he had all sorts of tubes coming from his stomach. Linda and I were for some reason the only children allowed on the ward. We would sit and sing to him 'Those Were The Days', or our other favourite of the time, 'Knock Knock Who's There?' Our little double act became well known along the beds, and when visiting Dad we'd often sing for the other patients too.

On the 5th April, the day before my birthday Dad came home. One of the first things he said to me was, 'Oh dear, I've really ruined your birthday.' I did not want to think of it that way. No I said, having him back home was the best present I could have wished for. The date for moving to the new house was now very close, and in view of Dad's frail state it was agreed the best thing was for him to go on ahead and stay with my older sister during all the upheaval and packing.

On the 14th of April we said goodbye to the prefab, and moved into Elmside, New Addington, where my dad joined us. Under any other circumstances it would have been a very happy and exciting occasion. But I knew my dad was seriously ill. The operation he had undergone following his collapse had confirmed he had cancer. Having been told there was nothing more that could be done, he had been discharged. For me, the day of the move was a terrible one, marking it seemed an irrevocable step, a step towards a dark chasm, something I barely understood, and even less wanted to think about.

My mother from necessity continued to go out to work, and when I arrived home from school each day there would be a period of about two hours when I would be the one looking after Dad. The downstairs of our new house had two main rooms, which were divided by partition doors. My dad, now sleeping much of the time, sat in an armchair in one room, while to let him rest I would stay in the adjoining room. If he needed anything, I would be close at hand. Since his voice was weak, his chair was placed next to the partition, which he could tap on at any time to summon me. Sometimes he would knock for a drink of water, occasionally for food, which he would attempt to eat, though he had no appetite, and his body weight was dropping dramatically.

For the whole two hours I would sit close to my side of the partition, perhaps with a book open or the TV on low, but all the while listening out for dad, to tap-tap for me to come to him. One day he and I had an ice cream together, which he really seemed to enjoy, as much for the act of us sharing it as anything. His breathing was laboured now, and a terrible rasping sound came from his lungs. 'If only I could stop this noise,' he would say to me, 'then I'd be all right.'

On the evening of the ninth day in the new house, I went up to bed as usual, only to wake up abruptly at a quarter past two in the morning screaming out the words, 'Daddy, don't die!' Then I looked up, and saw at the end of my bed my nun. 'It is time,' she said, 'be prepared.'

On waking again the following day I was informed that my dad had passed away in the night, his recorded time of death 2.15 a.m.

Eight

When Dad died he weighed just five stone. The cancer had consumed him at a vicious pace. A week after his passing an ambulance turned up at the house. The crew said they had come to collect a gentleman from our address to take him to hospital, and gave Dad's name. Somewhere or other, someone had made a mistake. It was a cruel one, turning the knife in the wound. His condition had actually been diagnosed back in March, when he had been given six months to live.

Everyone knew doctors could be wrong, with people sometimes living years longer than expected, and Dad the Miracle Man had defied the odds before. This time though, it had been the other way round, the six months had turned out to be a mere two, and he had spent just ten days in his new home. I had no experience of death. I remembered when I was about four years old, a black car came to the house, and everyone had been sad. Though I barely knew her, my grandmother had lived with us somewhere upstairs. After that day she wasn't there any more. Now the black car had come for my dad.

In the weeks that followed I sat for long periods downstairs, close to the partition, just as I had when looking after Dad. I thought of the day we had shared the ice cream, our last together, such a simple thing, but one that meant such a lot. On one occasion, hearing a tapping sound, I jumped up and went automatically into the adjoining room. The sound recurred often, and each time I would get up and go around the partition, finding only Dad's empty armchair.

My mother, having previously buried two sons, had now lost the only other male in her life, and was taking it very hard. My older sister's husband, seeing how upset I was, decided one day to take me aside and give me some advice. Rather sternly, he ordered that I was not to cry, 'for your mum's sake.' I was being made to feel it was wrong to be upset. But if I couldn't cry over my dad, then however could I even begin to bear this awful thing? Completely isolated and in such pain, with my mother wrapped up in her own despair, I felt desperate for someone to understand what I was going through, but no one was even listening.

I was wrong though. Someone was listening. It was about two weeks after my father's death, and I had gone down with the flu. I was lying in bed crying one night, when I began to sense a presence in the room. Was it my nun I wondered, come to tell me something awful again? Surely there could be no more terrible prediction than what had already come to pass. Then I heard a voice. It was not my nun, but someone much more familiar. It was my dad. He spoke softly. 'Don't cry sweetheart,' he said, 'we will be together again.' I couldn't answer, just stared at him, standing there so real, by my side just as he always had been. I noticed he had something in his hand, which he was holding out towards me. It was a box of Roses chocolates. "Tell Mum Happy Birthday", he said, 'and that I love her, and I haven't forgotten her.' His image then faded and I was alone in the room once more. Dad had always looked after me when I was ill, even if it was just putting his head round the door to check I was OK. Tonight he had shown me that nothing had changed.

The 7th May was my mum's birthday. On the day, my older sister came to visit, presenting her with a box of Rose's chocolates no less, just like the one I had seen carried in Dad's hand a few nights before. It seemed he had got his message to my sister as well. I said to Mum, 'That's what Dad gave you, when he came to me.' Neither my mum, nor my sister took much notice.

As spring blossomed and gave way to glorious summer, there was little of the joy these seasons usually bring. All I could dwell on was the horrible absence in my life - there would be no long trips with Dad in the lorry this year, nor ever again. And the thought of going to Leysdown without him, where every sight and sound - the walks on the beach, the music from the clubhouse, and the smell of the sea - would remind me of our happy times together, brought nothing but tears to my eyes.

I longed for him to visit me again at night, or any time, just to hear his voice or feel him with me. At home I could still hear his gentle tap tapping on the partition, and my mind was always distracted now. I could not seem to return to normal life, whatever that was, and would sit for hours at the top of the stairs, staring into space, lost in a trance. I had also been walking in my sleep. Looking out into the garden at night, I would see a shining light in the distance and try to walk towards it. If only I could reach the light I would think, if only I could get to it, then I would find my dad there.

The summer of 1969 came and went, and the autumn winds blew. The last year of the decade was drawing to a close. On Christmas morning I woke excitedly expecting Santa Claus to have been. Looking down at the end of my bed I saw my presents. All I could find was a hairbrush and a pair of tights. Surely this couldn't be right, I thought, Santa must have forgotten me. Perhaps he had accidentally missed our street.

When I looked outside and saw other children playing with brand new, proper presents, I knew it was only me who had been left out. Why? It must be because I had done something bad. Unusually for my age, I still believed in Santa Claus, not knowing it had always been my dad who had silently played the part, creeping into the bedroom as I slept and leaving presents. Now there was only Mum to make a careless, last minute gesture, with a cheap hairbrush and a pair of her own tights.

For me that Christmas morning marked both the beginning and end of something in my life. The mould that was still my childhood had started to crack, and with it all my innocence.

Nine

I had not been present during my dad's burial. Later on however, when I visited to lay flowers, although I had not been told whereabouts in the large cemetery his grave was located, I somehow found it straightaway.

Having been directed to Dad's resting place, I was now being made aware of a departed soul from further back in time. I had begun to have some very compelling dreams. Frequently these concerned a man I had never met, my father's father. The little I knew of my granddad was that he had been born in a workhouse, possibly, going by family anecdote, in the Shoreditch area of London. In my dreams I would see a large, rather forbidding looking building, a Victorian style edifice, possibly a hospital or similar institution. Suddenly I would find myself spirited within the walls, walking down long corridors, past endless doors and rooms leading off. Everything was a shade of drab green, walls, floors, ceilings, all the same. Throughout the dream it felt like I had become my granddad, seeing and hearing everything through his eyes and ears as it happened.

Two words came into my head and kept repeating: Sacred Heart, which sounded like the name of a hospital. I searched in London, but the only Sacred Heart Hospital was out in Epsom. Nevertheless I had a hunch about the place, and told my older sister, who was also interested in our granddad. She wasn't so sure about Epsom though, as there was no family link there. I was now getting stronger feelings than ever about this hospital, and persuaded my older sister that we pay a visit and see what we could uncover.

As soon as we arrived outside the hospital I said, 'I know this place - I've been here before.' My older sister replied immediately that it was impossible; neither I nor anyone else in the family had been there, so I couldn't even have picked up on someone else's recollections. I wondered if what happened in the dreams was occurring right now - my grandfather's eyes becoming mine, mine his, our spirits interconnecting on entering the proximity of the old building. Transported back in time, had I suddenly become him?

Swept along by this feeling I walked briskly through the main entrance. Seeing what looked like an office, I knocked on the door and marched straight in. My older sister followed close behind, apologising for me and trying to slow down my excited chatter as I explained to the woman registrar behind the desk, the reason for our visit.

After listening to the account of my dream, and of how I had been directed to the hospital, the registrar looked at me curiously for a moment. Possibly she was trying to weigh up my sanity. She was very kind however, and admitted to being fascinated by the story. Agreeing to see what could be found out, she asked for my grandfather's name and an approximate date, and bidding us take a seat, disappeared from the office. A few minutes later she returned. 'You were correct,' she announced, 'your grandfather was here. He died in this hospital over sixty years ago. According to the records he had an epileptic fit.'

My sister stared at me open mouthed, clearly amazed at how my dream had guided us to somewhere never known of or mentioned within the family, and quite removed from the area we had grown up in. She asked the registrar if anyone knew where our grandfather was buried. Unfortunately, replied the registrar, she didn't have that information. Then thinking for a moment, she suggested that someone who might be able to help, by looking in the parish records was the local vicar. She telephoned him, explained our request, and in a short while he arrived at the hospital.

The vicar had a long chat with us, asking how we had traced our grandfather to the Sacred Heart Hospital. I told him about the dreams, and how the name had kept repeating in my head. He nodded all the while, but explained that our methods of enquiry regarding a deceased forbear were not the 'normal' way of going about things, and seemed to find my story rather far fetched. It was a little awkward. He then said I appeared to be in 'rather a depressed state', and in an appeal to my older sister's seniority, suggested she take me home. If he found any information he would then write to us.

I was gripped however by a strong sense of determination, the same insistent feeling, accurate as radar that had led me to the hospital. Something was guiding me, telling me to press on. I could not go back. 'No,' I said, 'I will find my grandfather.' Both the vicar and my sister looked at me. 'He is here. I will show you his grave,' I said. 'Then you will believe me.' There was silence for a few seconds, then my older sister turned to the vicar. 'Would it be OK for us to have a drive around the grounds?' she asked. He looked slightly dubious, then said, 'It's not usual - but all right, if you wish. I'll come with you.'

The hospital was set in large grounds, to one side of which was a field. It was as we drove slowly past the field that something tugged at my mind. I had seen two tall trees, standing together in the distance. 'Stop!' I shouted. 'He's here.' Jumping from the car I began walking across the field. I passed the trees and a little further on felt the urge to stop. I looked around. It was just a random spot in the field. There was no gravestone or mounded earth, no sign of anything, just long grass and wild flowers waving gently in the breeze. There was a deep sense of deep there under the open sky, with the two trees a little way away like silent sentinels, their arms stretched towards heaven. Hearing a sound I turned and saw that the vicar had followed me across the field. 'This is the place,' I said. 'My grandfather is right here.' The vicar looked at me. 'Many years ago,' he said, 'this plot of land we are standing on was the hospital cemetery.' He then came and stood beside me in prayer. On the way back to the hospital office he said, 'I believe you now. There is no way you could have known about the cemetery being there.'

Before we left, my sister made one comment to him. 'The thing is vicar,' she said, 'she's in love with a ghost.' The phrase stuck in my mind. I realised in a way she was right. It had been an emotional impulse that had kept me searching, the need to somehow connect with my dear dad's dad, the blood tie and the spiritual bond calling me, till the quest brought us together at his final resting place. After that day I had no more dreams of my grandfather or the hospital. The quest was over.

The experience did make me think about other members of my dad's family who had long since passed to spirit, people who like my granddad I had never met. I could remember hearing vague snippets about some of these people, but had no idea what had become of any of them. What contact there had been with my father's side of the family, seemed to have been lost. I asked my older sister, but all she knew was that they were Londoners like us.

Then some time after Dad's passing, we received a phone call to say Dad's brother Nobby had died. At Nobby's funeral, during the wake, I finally got the chance to meet several of my dad's family I had never set eyes on before. I was also to learn something about Dad. Amid the hubbub of conversation I heard one lady talking about someone called Alice, who it was thought would be 'very sad' to know Nobby had died. Who was Alice? None other than Nobby's wife; apparently the pair had lived apart for some time and it hadn't been possible to contact her. I asked if perhaps I could get in touch, at which they all shook their heads. No one knew of her whereabouts. So while we all sat mourning the man who'd played a big part in her life and she in his, she remained blissfully unaware he was gone. She could go to her own grave not knowing. Who for that matter knew if she herself was alive or dead?

It was an odd situation, and there was something else baffling about it. Later I found out that Alice's surname was Tregent, but our family name on my dad's side was O'Neil. If she really were his brother Nobby's wife, why I wondered wasn't her surname the same? I asked my older sister but she didn't know either.

The mystery intrigued me. Back home I took the phone book and began trawling through the names. There were a few Tregents listed, but one in particular just stood out at me, and I had to call. When a woman's voice answered, I apologised for ringing out of the blue, but I was trying to trace an Alice Tregent. She said yes, she was Alice – who was I? Although we had never met, I said, as far as I knew I was her niece. She confirmed she had been married to my dad's brother Nobby, and it was then I broke the news to her. As the mourners had predicted she was deeply saddened. Alice and I exchanged further phone calls and a little later on we all met up as a family and talked about Dad and Nobby. The connection had been made.

There was one piece of the puzzle still missing though, the question of Alice's surname. This was where Dad came into the story. It turned out his surname had originally been Tregent. However being very close to his mother, and wishing to retain her memory, he had taken her maiden name as his own, O'Neil, which of course became our family name when he married Mum. His brother Nobby had stuck with their father's name, Tregent, which it turn became Alice's on their marriage.

Ten

My new school was called Fairchild High. As a fresh face in the playground, it was perhaps natural to be stared at by the other children. In my case there were other things to provoke interest. At home or school, since Dad's passing I continued to dress daily in black. This I suppose made me stand out, especially among the more fashion conscious girls in my year, like me were fast approaching their teens. And whenever my mother put in an appearance at the school gates, she was unusual among the other mums in that she was by now in her fifties, and it was often assumed she was actually my grandmother.

Soon it was also common knowledge I had no father, which invited certain pupils to jump gleefully to conclusions. In those days, anyone who didn't have a dad must be one thing and one thing alone, and once the rumour had started there was no stopping it. The taunts of 'bastard' were either hissed behind my back, or more frequently yelled in my face. Confronted with this behaviour, to try to explain about my dad would have been useless, and in any case I felt I did not want to. To have his name sullied by association with such poisonous, uncaring people would be quite wrong, and a gross injustice to my lovely dad, especially since I never stopped hoping and praying that he would somehow stay with me, and was even now watching over me.

The other thing that set me apart was my behaviour. Sitting in class my mind would often be elsewhere, listening to spirit, praying to my anonymous, unseen friend for guidance, or just some kind of solace. As in my primary school, I would only be awakened from these trance-like states by a shout from the teacher that I was 'away with the fairies again', followed by loud laughter all round.

But there was another side to my 'strangeness', which I learned, could be used to my advantage. While children made jokes about my mum, called out 'bastard' or referred to me as mad, I would sometimes tell them things about themselves – describe their homes, reel off the names of their relatives and even what their pets were called – things I could not possibly have known in the ordinary way. I would also tell them things about the future, which they did not know what to make of. Hearing these pronouncements would take them aback for a moment or two, the taunts would fall silent and they would look at me in a different way, uncertain how to respond. Sometimes a small group would trail round after me in the playground, some curious to know more, others just joining in what they saw as an enjoyable game. After a while though, with nothing more to say, they would resort to mockery again, laughing at me behind my back. Often I would see them make the gesture of pointing their index finger at their head then winding the finger round and round, the universal playground sign for 'she's round the twist.'

My sister Linda was also now at Fairchild High School. Whilst I was still the introvert, Linda was the noticeable extrovert, and very much Miss Popular, with lots of friends in her year. But she was also prone to arguments, and, being swift to hit out, often in trouble for fighting. At the same time, hidden by her tough outward nature, Linda had a vulnerable core. She too had been affected by Dad's death, but in a way she probably didn't realise, and that neither of us could understand She was desperate for affection, and craved hugs and cuddles, any contact or expression of warmth that would make her feel wanted and secure. In short, she needed the kind of love that both of us did, and which, sad but true had always seemed so sorely lacking in our mum.

Lately in fact Mum had been showing signs of change, though not in the way Linda or I would perhaps have wished for. The most visible alteration was to her appearance, particularly her clothes. Where before she would dress in nice, modest, traditional skirts and blouses, now she would often be seen in a mini skirt and long white boots. Dad would have hated it. But then she wasn't doing it for him. Mum began going out to bingo with her girl friends, and now and again, on the odd night, to the pub. Soon it was more than the odd night, and they got later. Sometimes I would go down and sit outside the pub she was in, waiting for her to emerge, looking up expectantly whenever there was a waft of ale and cigarette smoke and the babble of raucous conversation signalled someone was leaving. It often became a toss up whether to go home alone or sit there till last orders.

Inevitably Mum was going to meet a man, either in the pub or somewhere else, and before long she was in a relationship. When that ended, she began another, and so it was to go on. Obviously she was in need of company and no one could blame her for that. As an adult and a widow, she was perfectly entitled to a social life, a few drinks, a few laughs - and a love life. This might all have been fine if she had been happy. But as time passed, it seemed as if all the nights out, the drinking and the casual men friends were only taking her further downhill. Not only was she unhappy, she was not even content, certainly not at home, where both Linda and I seemed more and more the bane of her life.

Soon, a night in the pub was not enough to drown Mum's sorrows, and now when she arrived home she would often open some strong barley wine and carry on, in more ways than one. On the nights she stayed in, she would usually have a few bottles to keep her company. If anyone commented on her drinking, she would say it was to help her sleep. True she often passed out, which wasn't a pleasant sight, but her behaviour before she reached that point was harder to bear. As she got drunker, she got nastier, and would say vicious, cruel things. If I were in bed she would come and find me, and deliberately wake me up, yelling how she had never wanted me, and that I had ruined her life by being born.

As a family we seemed caught in a whirlpool of blame, guilt and hopelessness, and there appeared no way out. I hated my life, but so did my poor mum. With no support and very little money, she was clearly in despair, and when this turned to anger she took it out on the nearest person, most often me. She had always been prone to her moods, but was now becoming almost a different person. She drank to forget her sorrows, then drink depressed her more, and so the vicious circle turned, grinding her and everyone else down with it.

With my older sister busy with her own family, at twelve years of age I was in the position of playing mum to my younger sister. For her part, Linda still tended to focus her frustrations outwards, with her many and often highly charged friendships, scrapes and fights. I on the other hand, began turning increasingly in on myself. Still very much grieving for my dad, I would often take myself off to a nearby church. I didn't go to the services. I would have felt too awkward. Instead I wandered in when no one was around and sat in the silence, sometimes praying, sometimes just surrendering to the stillness of the place. 'Be still and know that I am God.' I suppose that's what I was doing.

At home I still spent many a late night sat on the stairs, or, in a trance, making my way towards the garden, drawn by the beacon of light that seemed to signal Dad's presence. If my mum wasn't too drunk or belligerent she would come and escort me back to bed, otherwise it would be Linda, who would gently take my arm and tell me I had been sleepwalking again. In class when I was laughed at for being 'away with the fairies' I used to say to myself 'if only', much better to be there, with the kind spirits, away where my dad was.

Caught between the lack of understanding at home and my tormentors – teachers and pupils – at Fairchild High, there seemed no place of escape. As the pressure mounted, something had to give, and it happened one morning while I was on my way to school. I was dreading the prospect of another day there and wanted to put off my arrival in the playground till the last possible moment, so to kill time before the bell I wandered off the beaten track, and down into a pedestrian underpass. It was an isolated place where not many people were seen during the day, though kids sometimes hung out after hours. I sat down and gazed up at the thick, solid structure that now surrounded me, like a bunker shutting out the world. The walls were made of huge, pre-formed slabs of concrete bolted together. There was lots of graffiti, spray-painted lettering, hearts with arrows linking names, swear words and crude drawings. Not exactly a beauty spot, but at least it was better than school, no one could get at me here.

After a few minutes, I began to cry, bitter tears of loneliness and utter misery. I was in such pain. Would it never go away? Raking my hand over the rough ground I felt something hard and sharp. I picked it up and saw it was a fragment of glass, part of a broken bottle. Still sobbing, I held the glass against my bare leg and pressed it gently, then a little harder then harder still, my whole body tense, till a warm, red liquid began to trickle through my fingers.

Eleven

I didn't go to school at all that day. I remained near the underpass, pacing to and fro or sitting, staring up at the sky and the grey concrete walls, till it was finally time to make my way home. My leg had not bled too much, though the wound was noticeable. The next morning I returned to the underpass and did the same thing, cutting myself again, then staying hidden there till home time. I knew if I went back to school the teachers would ask why I had been absent. What could I tell them? I had no idea. All I did know was that I would be in trouble if I didn't have an explanation. When children were off ill they were expected to have a note from their parents, but there was no way I could ask my mum to write one. Though she drank, smoked and gambled to excess, she was also very religious and upright when it came to her children's behaviour, and there would be hell to pay if she found out I was truanting, let alone asking her to lie for me. I was on my own.

I decided to compose a sick note myself, but sign it with my older sister's name. For some reason I felt this would be less risky, possibly I was worried the teachers might know Mum's handwriting. When I arrived at school and presented the note, my teacher looked at it closely, then at me. She seemed suspicious, but gave me the benefit of the doubt. It wasn't the last note I had to write. Every few days, when the bullying at school was too much for me, I would slink away to my secret place where, hidden amidst the concrete and graffiti, I would sit and weep, or find some glass to cut with. I had started on my arms as well as legs now. Why I did it I wasn't sure. The pain was quick and intense, and unlike the pain of my loneliness, I could decide whether or when it came, or didn't. Unlike everything else in my unhappy life, it was something I could control.

Now too, the bewildering onset of adolescence, when girls in particular start worrying about their appearance and sense of worth, wasn't helping my state of mind. Neither was my mum. She had been working shifts in a factory, in between cleaning in various private houses, where she would help herself to any alcohol that happened to be in her employers' fridges. With no let-up in her drinking, the effects were souring her like acid in milk. She began to step up the

42

unpleasant mind games with me. If the subject of relationships came up, she would turn on me with sarcastic comments like 'Who'd want you?' Perhaps in despising me my mother was despising herself. If I had any shred of self-esteem left at that point, this would have been enough to destroy it. Home was as unloving and hostile as school, and I couldn't bear to be in either place. Peering at my scrawled sick notes, my teachers would give me funny looks and say, 'Did you write this?' I would shake my head nervously, wondering what words I might have misspelled. The irony was I really was unwell, if only someone, somewhere could see it. The only friends I had were my spirits, but how could they help me in the everyday world? Lately the church too had become a place of fear, the fear of judgement. I was after all, wicked. The only refuge remaining for me was the underpass, with a shard of glass, and the power to inflict my own suffering.

Of course I had to be at home for some of the time, though I was always in dread of Mum having one of her outbursts, especially when she came back from the pub. One day though, it must have been almost a year after Dad had gone, she called Linda and I into the living room and said we were all going to have a quiet evening in together for a change. She put the radio on softly, found some books for us to read, and we all settled down. After a while I became drowsy. I looked across at Mum, who had her eyes half-closed. My head was aching, and suddenly I felt my stomach churning. Thinking I might be sick at any moment, I got up and went to open the lounge door. For some reason though it seemed to be locked, and I noticed there were some clothes pushed up against it on the floor. Trying the other door that led to the kitchen, I found clothes barring my way here too. Dragging the things away, I managed to tug the door open and stumbled out, followed closely by Linda, who was also feeling queasy A few seconds later my mum came rushing into the kitchen to find us. She grabbed hold of me and then Linda and hugging us both very tightly, burst out crying. Dropping to her knees, tears still pouring down her cheeks she sobbed, 'I'm sorry, I'm so, so sorry, I didn't mean it, I'm sorry…!'

Neither Linda nor I realised what had really happened that day. We just thought Mum was having one of her turns. Not till years later would it dawn on us that she had tried to gas us all. In a moment of madness, she had tried to take herself and her children away from it all for good. Looking back it showed not only the terrible low ebb she had sunk to, but also that she did have a conscience. Without my knowing it, tugging at the door may have awoken her at the crucial moment, and her heart, or God, something, had spoken and she knew what she was doing was wrong.

Occasionally mum showed a glimmer of concern, an impulse to do something nice. Maybe it was remorse after the incident with the gas stove, that made her feel obliged to try and help me out one day, if indeed that's what she thought she was doing. It happened while I was visiting her for some reason at the factory, when I saw, working alongside her a young man. I'll call him B. In the course of conversation Mum sort of introduced us. Perhaps she thought someone might want me after all, if only as a friend, he being seventeen and I a mere thirteen. B seemed to take an interest in me; though little did I know at the time where it would lead.

The months went by, and our lives rattled on in their familiar, shambling way, Mum drunken and moody, me still feeling generally low and slipping off school, still harming myself from time to time.

I was also having some vivid dreams and premonitions. One night I dreamt that three little children we did not know came to live in our house with us, such a strange idea that I couldn't make head or tail of it. It's meaning would soon be revealed however. My older sister, whose successful marriage had seemed the only fixture in our family, had now split up with her husband, and been left to bring up two children on her own. Recently she had become friendly with our milkman, and would make a point of being around to chat and flirt with him when he came by. She got so eager, that at six a.m. one morning when there was no sign of him, she sent me up the road to check on his whereabouts.

Soon the milkman and my older sister were having a relationship, and planning to live together. Meanwhile they asked my mum a favour: while the domestic arrangements were being sorted out, would she mind if the milkman's kids stayed at our house for a while? My mum agreed, and so it was that three young children came to live with us, just as my dream had foretold.

Coinciding with my visions, I was still experiencing both sleepwalking and insomnia. This, and the fact that I kept telling people about my spirit visitors was causing growing concern within the family. My mother fretted about the sleepwalking, in as much as it got on her nerves and woke her up in the night. This all got back to my older sister, who took it upon herself to do something about me. After first visiting my doctor, an appointment was made for me to see someone at a place called the Crescent Day Hospital. My older sister came along with me and sat there while the psychiatrist gave a long spiel and they both talked about me - not being able to sleep, my mum, and about my dad dying - which the psychiatrist seemed to think was very important. To me, it just felt like they were trying to confuse me. I was prescribed sleeping pills and anti-depressant tablets, and told I must come back to the Crescent every day from now on. It was a routine I soon got into. What I was expecting from the treatment I didn't really know. Presumably the combination of pills and therapy were intended to make life dull but calm for me from now on. What fate had in store for me however, was quite the reverse.

Seeing a shiny motorcycle parked in the street one day, and thinking it was familiar, I went up to take a closer look. Then I thought I might try sitting on it. As I was about to I heard someone shout, 'Aye you - get off my bike!' It was B. It was almost a year since I had first met him at Mum's workplace. Now here he was swaggering out of the pub. I realised he must be well over eighteen by now. He had recognised me of course, and deliberately spoke in that knowing, provocative way that lads of that age often do. Walking straight up to me he said, 'Come on give us a kiss then'. Instinctively I stepped back off the pavement. 'No,' I said, 'No.'

Later on we did kiss and before long I seemed to have become his girlfriend, him eighteen, me fourteen. Oh well, it was only kissing.

I was lucky to have one really good female friend, my best friend in fact. Her name was Sally, and one day she invited me to her birthday party. I was really pleased to be going, but my only concern was getting home on time, since, if ever I were late in, Mum would go absolutely spare, shouting at me and calling me names, assuming I was out with boys and doing things I shouldn't. However Sally had invited her guests for early evening, and not being too far away I could either return by bus or walk home.

The party was fun, with records and dancing, and everyone seemed to be having a good time, me included. Worried about Mum though I didn't stay too long. After saying goodbye to Sally, I had just started walking down the road when a van pulled up sharply beside me at the kerb. The window wound down and music came thumping out. It was my boyfriend B. He had got rid of his motorbike.

'Where you off to?' he said.

'Home' I replied, carrying on walking.

'Jump in, I'll give you a lift.'

I said my mum didn't like me accepting lifts, and would have a go at me if she saw me arrive home with someone. He said it would be OK, as my mum knew him. I hesitated for a moment and looked up the road. The time was already getting on. If I couldn't get a bus straightaway it would be gone ten before I got home, and Mum would not be best pleased. The door of the van swung open, and I got in. As we revved off down the road, B jabbed a finger at the stereo. The track changed to 'You Can Get It If You Really Want.' It was a favourite of his.

I was tired after the party, and didn't notice at first that we were taking a different route to my house. Only when everything went quiet did I realise we had stopped somewhere.

'Come on, let's have a cuddle', said B. nodding towards the back of the van and the old sofa he kept there. We had cuddled and kissed on it before. I wasn't particularly keen to go home and face Mum, who would probably be on the warpath about me staying out late anyway by now. We settled on the sofa and B began kissing me. His hands were everywhere and he kept trying to get me to lie down. As I tried to push his hands away he took hold of my wrists and held them tight. The next minute he was lying on top of me.

'B, get off, you're squashing me,' I said.

'Just lay still,' he said, 'I'm just going to lay it there OK.'

'No, I don't want to, you're hurting me, stop, stop please…!'

I tried to squirm out from beneath him, but he had me pinned firmly down.

Then as he shifted, I felt a sudden, searing pain. For several minutes he lay across me, his body a heavy, suffocating weight as he raped me.

When it was over he climbed back behind the wheel and said he would drive me home. I cried all the way.

As we pulled up outside the house he told me not to let my mum see I was upset. 'Don't tell her anything,' he said, 'or she'll lock you away.' I wanted to die.

I walked into the living room and saw Mum sat in the chair. She had been drinking. 'And where do you think you've been?' she snarled. 'Look at the time!'

Unable to speak I just looked down at the floor. 'You little tart!' she yelled, and marched to the kitchen, returning with a bucketful of water. She threw the whole lot over me, drenching me from head to toe.

I went upstairs and took off my wet clothes, then got into bed and cried myself to sleep.

Twelve

The following summer it was time for me to leave school, and not a moment too soon as far as I was concerned. I was relieved to be getting away from the place for good, away from the heartless bullies who had called me 'bastard', and the teachers who knew everything about history and geography and maths, but nothing of the spirit world that for me was so real. Free at last, the only question was, what on earth was I going to do now?

The obvious answer was I had to get a job. It was 1972, and throughout Britain, with strikes, power cuts and a three-day week looming, not the best of times to be looking for work. Even in a recession though there were things people always wanted, one of them being footwear, and when I saw a vacancy for a sales assistant in a nearby shoe shop, I went along for an interview. The boss, a chap in his forties, seemed very friendly, and offered me the job at a weekly wage of £8.20.

For the first few days, it was a case of learning the ropes; manly the layout of the shop and the stock. Among the popular styles were Wedges, big platforms, and Hush Puppies, the ones in the adverts with the floppy eared dog and big soulful eyes. Once I had helped customers try on and select their shoes, they would take them over to an elderly lady with bright red fingernails who sat at the cash desk. Also working in the shop were a young looking twenty-two year old girl, and two sisters of nineteen and twenty. Both the sisters had beautiful hair, hated the job and spent most of their time talking to each other. The other member of staff was a female supervisor, who always seemed to be going off somewhere. The boss himself was rarely around either and frequently he and the supervisor would disappear together.

Though I had been very withdrawn at school, the experience of being among people here was so different, especially with the customers. I enjoyed meeting them, having a chat and helping them find what they wanted, getting out all the boxes so they could try on different sizes and colours. There was something about buying new shoes that seemed to bring people out, something upbeat about with it, which was catching. Their cheerfulness made me happy. The other girls were more than content to let me get on with it, and some days I was the only one doing any selling. Soon I was shifting more stock overall than anyone else.

One morning a lady came in to the shop and asked to see the boss. I said he had been in earlier but had to go out somewhere. Afterwards one of the other girls told me it was his wife. She came in often, and always her husband was absent, usually at the same time as the supervisor. It didn't take a genius to put two and two together.

When I had been there six months the boss took me aside. He told me I had done really well, and therefore would be receiving a pay rise the following week. Sure enough, in my next wage packet instead of £8.20 there was £11.20. Not bad I thought for a fifteen year old, and in my first job too. I really loved it too. For the first time in years I felt special.

I was still seeing B, my boyfriend. I had never told anyone about what happened in his van. I had been scared to – scared of him, of my mum knowing, and other people too, scared of what might happen. Because he was older, or just made that way, B would always tell me what to do. Disliking arguments, it seemed easier most times to go along with his wishes. With certain issues though this was more difficult. Though he knew something of my emotional problems, he was not exactly sympathetic, and made it clear he disliked the fact I was seeing a psychiatrist. Several times he told me that his friends and family would think I was 'mad', and that I should stop going to the sessions. This was not so simple since I was still 'under the doctor'. The situation was complicated still further by the fact that my boyfriend's family were friends with my older sister, who had taken me to the Crescent day hospital in the first place. There seemed no way of keeping all of them off my back at the same time.

B was becoming not only more controlling, but aggressive too. He was also it turned out, a snob. When this side of his personality reared its head, it was to smash the one bit of pride and happiness I had found. He dropped the bombshell with the request, or more like order, that I should stop working at the shoe shop. He didn't want any girlfriend of his, he said, to be in 'such a low job.' I was very upset at the idea of leaving the shop, but whether through lack of confidence, insecurity, or because I felt he might be right in some way I couldn't understand,

I found it hard to challenge him in the matter. I therefore acquiesced, and shortly after gave in my notice. Naturally the boss was surprised, and I didn't know quite what to tell him.

I applied to a firm called SEGB, who were looking for girls to be key-card punch operators. I had to sit some tests before they would take me on, and since I had left school without much in the way of qualifications, I didn't feel too confident about this. The tests however proved an eye-opener for me. I found I could do them, could understand what was required, answer the questions and solve the various problems set. Having always been dismissed by my teachers and my mother as 'away with the fairies' etc, etc, to actually pass these aptitude tests, it began to dawn on me that I might have ability after all, that I might even be, dare I say it, bright.

There were no customers as such, only the other girls to talk to; in fact men were apparently not allowed to work in our section. I soon adapted to the new environment and enjoyed acquiring skills. After the key cards I was trained to use CMC tape and an IBM 127 machine, at that time the latest thing in computing. Soon I didn't really miss the shoe shop. I got to hear some of the gossip though; the nice boss there and his supervisor had both been given the sack. Presumably word of their long lunch hours together had got to the ears of head office.

By this time my sister Linda had also left school, and had a job as an accounts clerk. She was also now going out with someone, her childhood sweetheart. Both being at work, Linda and I were companions again, taking the bus into Croydon together in the mornings, and meeting up in town for lunch, which we really enjoyed.

Whether my new position was less of a 'low job' in my boyfriend's eyes I wasn't sure, but at least he couldn't say I hadn't done as he asked. If I thought this was going to ensure me a quiet life though, I was mistaken.

As regards my mum, I was about to discover something about her, something she had hitherto kept secret, but which would now ignite in me a burning curiosity. Coming home early from work one day, I found her sat round the kitchen table with a couple of her female friends. There was nothing unusual about this as she often had people in for tea. There was something else going on though. They seemed to be in a huddle, and Mum was staring intently into her cup. Though

I had never seen it before, I seemed to know in a flash what it was
- she was reading the tealeaves. When she realised I was there, and
watching her, she stopped abruptly. Obviously she hadn't expected
me home.

Later on I broached the subject, and asked her if she would do a
reading for me. After some hesitation she made a brew, took a cup,
and looked into it, her eyes narrowing. I waited breathlessly to hear
what would be revealed. Suddenly her face was filled with fear and
in a rush of emotion she thrust the leaves away. 'No, no,' she cried, 'I
can't, I can't…!'

Thirteen

What my mother had seen in the tealeaves she would not say. Perhaps there was nothing. Or was it something so horrible, so appalling, that she could not bear to contemplate it, let alone reveal it to me? Not sharing that knowledge would be a way of having power over me. On the other hand, maybe she really did fear for me in what she had seen. Afterwards when she had calmed down and the teacup was washed and put away out of sight she turned to me and said, 'You're psychic you know.'

This acknowledgment, like seeing her do the reading, was a first for me. Till then all my talk of dreams and visitations and predictions had only been met with cross words and warnings of hellfire punishments. My grandfather, a staunchly religious and God-fearing man, may have instilled in her a deep fear of anything that smacked of 'the devil's work'. I remembered how right from when I was small Mum would scold me vehemently if I dropped the Bible during our evening prayers. Now I knew she not only had psychic ability, but an overwhelming sense of guilt about it at the same time. Was this why she had tried to smother and deny the same thing in me? Though I couldn't really understand it at the time, the tension between my mother's natural gifts and the strictures of religion may well have offered a clue to her contradictory personality.

Her seeming lack of love for me was matched by an irresponsible attitude, an almost complete absence of practical, everyday care. When I got home from work I would, as always, do the housework. Mum was either still on shift at the factory, upstairs with her man friend or out drinking, and therefore rarely cooked a meal for me. I was thus either obliged to find something for myself in the kitchen, or make other arrangements.

Then one day other arrangements were made for me. It was my boyfriend, who by this time was my fiancé, who did the arranging. How I had agreed to marry him I don't know, but now everyone just assumed that was the way it was to be. I was always afraid to say otherwise. B didn't like me having any friends, male or female, and would constantly question me about my movements, and whom I had seen or spoken to. Probably he thought if I talked to other people they might put ideas in my head.

As B's wife-to-be, it was only to be expected things would start as they were meant to go on, and so from now on it worked like this; after finishing the housework in my own home, I would go round to my B's mother's house and do the cleaning there. In return for these chores, my future mother-in-law would provide me with dinner. It was good to have a regular evening meal, though not so good to be slipping further under B's watchful and controlling eye.

If only it had stopped there. My boyfriend was a heavy drinker, and as with my mum, this did not make him a nice person. The first time he hit me it was a tremendous shock. When it happened again, and in my own home, I could still barely take in what was happening. Not only had he raped me at the age of fourteen, but this man, whom my mum had introduced me to, the person I was expected to marry no less, was a thoroughly nasty, possessive and violent character. How could I possibly carry on seeing him? Then again, how could I not? Cleaning his house, eating at his table and barely allowed out of his sight, while in constant fear of his temper and his fists, I was bound hand and foot to him.

There seemed little chance of help from within the family. My older sister, if she knew what was going on, was seemingly turning a blind eye to it. Mum too couldn't seem to care less, even when the abuse was happening under her nose. Perhaps they both dismissed the shouting and my crying, and the bruises that followed, as 'domestic disputes' in which it was best not to interfere. Often my boyfriend would physically abuse me while my mum was well within earshot, upstairs with her own man. A fat lot she cared, being well away on drink herself. If I cried out, her man would stamp loudly on the bedroom floor and shout. 'Tell him to go, tell him to go!' This just made my boyfriend more aggressive.

One evening though, the situation got too much even for my mum to ignore. My sister Linda, the only one who would stick up for me, was in the room when he started on me, hitting and punching my face. As I tried to get away, Linda yelled out, 'He's killing Tina, Mum, he's killing her!' at the top of her voice. The next moment my mother came downstairs, grabbed a carving knife from the kitchen, and pointing it at my boyfriend screamed, 'Leave her alone!'

The following morning I waited till B had slunk off, and then went in to work as usual. My boss, noticing the big blotches on my face, came up and asked if I was all right. I nodded but didn't say anything. That night I prayed as I often did. Prayed for a way out, for help, for guidance. I thought of my wonderful, kind dad, and all the happy times we had shared, and how much I loved him. How sad he would be to see me all alone and so afraid now. If only he were here I thought, to say a comforting word, or give me his fond smile of reassurance as only he could. Perhaps after all he was watching, biding his time till the moment when he could speak to me, waiting for a chance to make things better.

Before I knew it I had turned eighteen. Apart from the noticeably violent flare-ups with B, like the night my mum brandished the carving knife, the family were still mostly blasé about his behaviour. They just didn't seem to want the aggravation, and to give them the slim benefit of the doubt, they may have thought they were acting in my interests by not further antagonising B.

My older sister did do one thing, which, indirectly, seemed her way of trying to help me. It involved a pen friend society, to which she already belonged. Members could write and receive letters from people in different walks of life, including boys in the armed forces. She arranged to put me in touch with three correspondents, one a young army lad another in the navy and one serving with the air force. I wrote off to them, but with little idea what to expect.

I had now been with B for nearly five years, during which time his violence towards me had only grown worse. From an occasional bout of punching and slapping, I was now being subjected to prolonged beatings on a regular basis. This made me continually anxious, and I would turn to prayer, as much as a form of meditation as for any hope of hearing answers. In the midst of the storm that battered around my head, often literally, prayer was a way of trying to still my mind.

I would often recall a verse from the Bible, which had been hung on my door as a child: 'I expect to pass this way but once: if therefore there be any kindness I can show, or any good thing I can do, let me do it now, let me not defer or neglect it, for I shall not pass this way again.' How these words could relate to me I did not know, but just keeping them in my mind seemed to help.

One day I received a letter. It was from a boy in the army, replying to my letter sent through the pen friend society. Shortly after I heard from two more, one in the navy and one in the air force. The army boy quickly followed up with several more letters, and said he wanted to meet me. From the tone of the letters, which were very over the top, I didn't think it wise to encourage him. My most regular correspondent became the one in the air force, whose name was Mal. He had sent me a small portrait photograph - so small in fact it was hard to see what he looked like, but from his letters he sounded like a nice person. It was like having a companion, but one who was outside of everything, not judging, just someone to talk to, like a friendly stranger on a train. I began to tell Mal everything that was going on with me, how my boyfriend hit me, and about my mum's drinking. I said I felt really awful and depressed a lot of the time, and didn't know what to do or where to go.

One day Mal wrote to tell me that although he was stationed down in Wales, and couldn't have people to stay on the base, if ever things got too desperate at home I could go and stay with his parents. At the bottom of the letter he had written their address. It was somewhere up in the Midlands, miles away. It was a nice gesture. The idea though of turning up on someone's doorstep, people I didn't know and asking for their help didn't seem like the kind of thing I could ever do, and anyway what would I do when I got there?

Not that I didn't think about running away. The only problem was where to run to. Much as I hated my home, it was still home, and a kind of security. There was also the worry over how B might react if I left him. Not only was I dependent, I felt afraid too, terrified of what he might do. One of his beatings had left me with a broken hand, and that was over something trivial. If I ran away I felt sure he would find me, and what punishment would follow then? It would mean getting right out of the area, out of London even, and leaving my job. I might get a few miles, but how long would I survive without money, a roof over my head? It always came back to the same thing, B. He seemed to have a hold over me, a power that I could not escape from.

Gradually though, a plan of some kind began to take shape in my head. In a safe place in the house I started squirreling away pound notes from my wage packet each week. I also found an old suitcase, dusted it off and tucked it out of sight but ready, in my room. Ready for what I wasn't sure exactly. I didn't have what you might call a long-term strategy The idea of Scotland, the wild northernmost part, kept coming into my mind, but that would probably use up most of my money on a train or coach, and what would I do when I got there? Perhaps after all I was crazy to even think about going anywhere.

It took one more night of hell at the hands of B to convince me otherwise. When everyone had gone out the morning after, I quickly and quietly packed a few clothes in my tatty suitcase, put the pound notes I had been saving carefully into my pocket, and after placing a scribbled note with the message 'I can't take it any more' on the kitchen table, left the house.

Hurrying down the road I felt conspicuous with my suitcase. My worry was that someone would stop me, or a nosey neighbour start asking where II was going. I halted at the bus stop, turning my face from passers by, pretending to peer in shop windows or fiddle with my case. When a double-decker came along bound for East Croydon railway station, I hopped on and hid myself in one of the downstairs seats. As the bus gathered speed and we left the estate behind, I relaxed a little and sat up to look out of the window. I had already abandoned the idea of Scotland, deciding instead to take up my pen friend's offer and try to find his parents. They lived in a place called Newark, up in the Midlands. I didn't know exactly how to get there, but felt sure that if I headed to London I could get a train from one of the big stations. Somehow I would get there. More daunting was what happened then – what I would say to these people and how they would react. Suppose they turned me away, or rang the police or the family found out my destination then called B, and he came to collect me? With these thoughts racing through my head, I became a bundle of nerves again.

Victoria Station was crowded with passengers criss-crossing in every direction as they hurried between platforms, weaving in and out of others stood still, staring up at the information boards or straining to hear the announcements. It was like seeing brief snapshots of hundred of lives – businessmen late for meetings, tired night workers and cleaners on their way home, people with flowers off to visit relatives in hospital, retired couples on a day out in London, schoolchildren shepherded by their teachers and tourists struggling with luggage, unsure where they were supposed to be going. Maybe that's what they thought I was, or with my tatty case, a refugee more like.

After some enquiries I found my way across London to St. Pancras. This was more bustling still, and the platforms seemed to go on forever. After buying my ticket and boarding the train for Newark, the reality of the situation, that I was about to throw myself on the mercy of people I had never met, hit me, and I spent much of the journey in a state of anxiety.

I needn't have worried. Mal's parents were lovely, and, appearing to understand the situation without me having to explain too much, said I was welcome to stay. That night though I felt very scared. I had never been away from home without my family before. Now I had cut myself completely adrift, it felt as if the ground was no longer under my feet. Lying awake in the strange room, amid unfamiliar surroundings, the world seemed suddenly so vast and lonely, and I had no idea what tomorrow would bring.

Fourteen

In the morning I thanked my hosts, and said I had better be on my way. When they asked where I was headed. I gave some vague reply, picked up my suitcase once again, and waved farewell to them.

On the train back to London I decided I would try to find Mal. It would of course have made sense if I had spoken to his parents about this while I was with them, and got his exact whereabouts. Perhaps I had felt they would disapprove. In any case I wasn't thinking 'sensibly'. Maybe there was a reason for that; I seemed to be following my destiny one step at a time, letting my instincts or some inner voice guide me.

Being in the air force and unmarred, Mal lived in service quarters, presumably behind barbed wire and sentries. All I really knew of the location was that it was somewhere in south Wales. It might take ages to discover, and even then, suppose he couldn't see me for some reason, or had been posted elsewhere at short notice? Whatever the outcome, the fact was I didn't know what else to do.

The train from London to Cardiff took a couple of hours, and all the way there I anxiously kept my fingers crossed. On arrival I found a telephone box, which in those days had the big phone directories hung beneath the receiver. I couldn't afford a hotel, so flipped through a few pages until, listed under 'Hostels' I saw the number of the Young Women's Christian Association. They said they had rooms for that night and gave me the address and directions of how to get there from the station. Once at the hostel I rang my older sister to let her know I was OK, and to pass on the message to Mum and Linda not to worry. After some hesitation, I also gave her the details of where I was staying.

The YWCA was £10 a week for board and lodging, which included breakfast and an evening meal, so I could afford to be there for a few weeks if need be. In the meantime I could perhaps try to get a job, and hopefully make contact with Mal. The only problem with the hostel was that you had to be out by 10 am each morning, and couldn't go back till 6 pm in the evening. For those girls that weren't in work, it meant finding somewhere to go during the day. In the summer this might have been easier, with the parks and streets to explore, but it was still only February with the weather either cold, or cold and wet, and I hadn't left home with the warmest of overcoats. My refuge became the indoor shopping centre, where I would spend most of the time trailing round gazing at the window displays, in between topping up on hot drinks in the Littlewoods cafeteria.

A couple of weeks went by. I knew I would have to do something eventually, get a job or find Mal, but for the present I seemed to want to just get through each day alone with my thoughts, hidden among strangers, far away from anyone that knew me. Every so often those thoughts turned to home, sometimes guiltily, or with curiosity, picturing my family going about their lives without me. One afternoon while in town I went to a phone box and called my older sister again, just to let her know I was still coping all right. It was a good job I did. She had some alarming news - B was intending to come down to Wales to find me.

With barely a goodbye I put down the receiver with trembling hands. Breathing rapidly I tried to think what to do next. How had B discovered my whereabouts? But this was no time to speculate. If he had an address, there was no doubt in my mind he would come looking for me there, and might be on his way even now. I had a sudden image of him sneaking his way into my room, cornering me there, out of sight and earshot, his face contorted with rage, his fists raised. Almost falling out of the phone box, I began running and didn't stop till I had reached the hostel. Flinging open my suitcase I crammed everything into it, shut the lid and raced from the building.

Once safely away from the hostel I realised I now had nowhere to stay. One option was to spend the night on the streets, hardly a pleasant prospect, especially at such a time of year. Besides there was always the chance my ex might stumble across me. Having given him the slip at the hostel, he was quite capable of trawling the whole town for me, his anger mounting with every step.

Feeling very vulnerable, in desperation I found my way to the nearest police station and spluttered out my story to the desk sergeant. He looked at me for a moment then said, 'Do you know anyone locally you can stay with?' I shook my head, but then told him about Mal, stationed in south Wales with the air force. The sergeant said he would see what could be done. After making some phone calls he got through to an RAF base, and gave Mal's name to the person on the other end of the line. Eventually Mal was found and told I had nowhere to stay, and had a violent ex-boyfriend on my trail. After a brief discussion it was arranged that Mal would come out and pick me from the police station that evening.

I wasn't sure what to expect on meeting Mal. His letters had always been pleasant and thoughtful, but I had only ever had the one tiny snapshot of him. When he arrived he had an air force colleague with him. They explained that as I wouldn't be allowed on the RAF base, I could stay with the colleague, who lived in married accommodation outside. Feeling a sense of relief, I watched my suitcase being loaded into the boot of Mal's car and off we drove. That night brought another strange bed in the home of a family I did not know. Like Mal's parents however they were kind and decent people, and though the future remained uncertain, I was at least safe.

After two weeks with Mal's colleague's family it was time to move again. The posting in south Wales for training had come to an end, and Mal was scheduled to return to his main base, which was away on the other side of the country, up towards the east coast. After talking things over it was agreed I would go along. I could only follow him so far though. As before I would not be permitted on the base, and this time there was no possibility of staying with any of his colleagues. The only affordable alternative was another hostel, the nearest being Ipswich. One YWCA was much like another. I was used to their rules and routines, and with the weather improving it was no hardship to spend the daytimes out and about now. When his duties allowed I could also see Mal now, and, in the months that followed, as we got to know each other, a relationship began to form.

I still kept in touch with my family back in New Addington. Mum it seemed was much the same, and my older sister busy with her own life with the milkman and their combined family. It was nice to talk to Linda. I was happy now to tell them all what I was up to, and where I was. There was always a danger that B might try to find me again, though as time went on I thought the possibility less likely.

I was in for another shock though. One evening, returning to the hostel at the usual time, I was told the manager wanted to speak to me. She said a young man had been in that day, asking where I was. I didn't need a description to know it was B. I had underestimated just how angry and obsessed he obviously still was, and all the old feelings of fear came rushing back. From his manner, the manager went on, the staff had sensed trouble, and out of concern for myself and the other girls it was felt best for everyone if I found alternative accommodation. It was a polite way of telling me to pack my suitcase, not that I needed any persuading.

After the hostel it was one crummy bed-sit after another. And B somehow seemed to know about all of them. By luck or judgment I always managed to evade him, but where was it going to end? I could keep moving, but if someone in the family was giving me away what was the use? The only choice seemed to be to cut myself off completely or be forever on the run.

Discussing the situation with Mal one day, we realised there was another option, a solution staring us in the face in fact, which if we chose to use it would give us both complete peace of mind about B once and for all. Mal had recently received notification that his squadron was to be disbanded, and he had been offered an alternative posting on a base up in North Norfolk. This base was very hush-hush being a vital missile site with top security and a perimeter fence guarded twenty-four hours a day. There was no way any unauthorised person could get within spitting distance of the place, be they friend or foe.

However if the 'friend' happened to be married to of one of the serving personnel it was an entirely different matter, for on this base there were special arrangements for spouses. Why didn't I become Mal's spouse? It was a big step, but things had progressed between us. As a legal couple we could live on the base together and I could go to sleep every night in probably the most secure place in Britain, ignoring a few hundred tonnes of explosive warheads lying around. The more we talked it through, the more it seemed the obvious thing to do.

There was one fly in the ointment - Mal's family. Mal and I had only known each other, apart from as pen friends a short time, and his parents were curious, not to say suspicious about me. On top of this was the fact they had lately lent Mal a significant sum of money, which, it had been agreed would be paid back. They now seemed worried he was rushing headlong into a marriage before sorting out his other responsibilities.

Hoping the conflict would be resolved we continued with our plans. Mal's parents however were serious about the matter, and dug in their heels, advising that if he went ahead with the wedding they would appoint a solicitor to recover the money he owed them. Were they determined their son should honour his commitments, or did they just not want him to marry me? Whatever the answer, it was a fait accompli as Mal simply didn't have the money. Finally, to solve the problem, Mal took out another loan, enabling him to pay his parents back in full and have done with it.

So it was that on the 10th April 1976, at a registry office in Stowmarket Suffolk, Mal and I were wed. Only four other people attended; my mum and my niece, whom Mal had collected from London, and two of his Royal Air Force buddies. Obviously Mal's parents were still not pleased about our union. After the ceremony, Mal and I went back to New Addington with my mum. Mal couldn't stay long, and so we agreed I would spend a few days with Mum and then go up to Norfolk to join him.

There was one nasty surprise to come. A week after Mal had left, B. turned up at my mum's house. He had heard all about my marriage and was coming for his revenge. He took it good and proper, putting me in hospital. I was advised to take him to court, but in the knowledge I would soon be away from south London, probably for good, I simply didn't want go through all that, I didn't have the heart. Free of him now, I wanted to put that part of my life firmly behind me.

I reflected on how strange it was to be at home again, and felt a flood of memories and emotions. Seeing the living room, I recalled my dad's last precious days, and how I had sat listening for his tap-tap on the partition, the ice cream we had shared and the smile it brought to his pitifully shrunken features, and how much I loved him. No one could ever take that away.

At barely nineteen, it felt like I already had more years than that of fretful existence behind me, what with my poor, frustrated, unhappy mum, a vindictive and bullying ex-partner, and the inexplicable inner misery that had driven me to despair and self-harm. Then there were the dreams and visitations, often disturbing, and the wistful longing for my dear dad and the wonderful times we had had together, missing him so much still.

Though Dad would always be special, and remain with me, outwardly and in other respects life had to move on. And so here I was, married to a man in uniform and serving his country, someone I had come to though the conversation of our written words. We got on well, and were now looking forward to setting up a home together. Perhaps there was such a thing as happiness after all.

Fifteen

Mal's posting with 85 Squadron was to RAF West Raynham in Norfolk. The base had been a centre of operations for Bomber Command during the Second World War, and lost eighty-six aircraft in the duration. Now it was 1976, and the Cold War with Russia - the fear that it might hot up at any time – meant the base was still important strategically. Being miles from anywhere and a non driver, strategically important for me was the one bus a day that ran to and from the nearest village of Fakenham; if you happened to miss it either end, you were stranded till the next day.

The change of environment and being married was obviously a whole new way of life for me. It took a while to adjust to the fact that I was now free from all kinds of worries - the fear of being pursued, the overbearing presence of my mum, and the general atmosphere of tension and agitation I had lived with were simply no longer an issue. There was also good news from my sister Linda, who, a little while after Mal and I tied the knot, had announced that she was to marry her childhood sweetheart.

With all these positive life changes for both me and for my loved ones, I found I stopped praying. Once upon a time, I had turned regularly to prayer in the face of anxiety and depression about what was going on around me, now I was simply getting on with life. The absence of prayer had in turn, other effects. Where before, prayers had stilled the spirit voices in my head, now they returned and spoke to me. The more I relaxed, the more I started tuning in again to what was unseen.

This was not always to be an agreeable experience, particularly as regards the house I was now living in. Like most old dwellings our accommodation had its share of creaky floorboards and relics, which here included fittings for the wartime blackout shutters still on the windows. But there was something else. From the moment I entered I had noticed a chill about the place. I realised this had nothing to do with the weather; even in summer the rooms felt cold, and upstairs the windows were sometimes iced over on the inside. Mal was aware of the strange atmosphere too. I also had the feeling we were being watched. During my time on the run I had got used to looking over my shoulder, but this was different.

Then one day I saw someone. It was a young boy, stood at the top of the stairs. He started appearing regularly, never speaking or moving, just standing there, waiting, watching. I knew clearly that he was an unhappy soul. I told Mal about it, and after a while we moved our bed to the ground floor, only going upstairs to use the bathroom. This was not only because it was warmer down below. I did not like seeing the boy on the stairs.

He was not to be ignored so easily however. When our doorbell rang one evening, I went to answer it but found no one there. The following day, hearing the rattle of the letterbox, I went into the hall expecting to find post for us but there was nothing on the mat. Both the doorbell and the letterbox repeated these tricks, ringing and rattling without explanation at various times of the day and night.

It was on a peaceful summer's day that a more alarming incident occurred, and it was our local farm butcher who found himself on the receiving end. Just as he was coming in the back gate with our weekly delivery, there was a loud crash. The window of our garden shed had blown clean out, hurling shards of glass over the path. The poor butcher was standing there amidst it all, staring in shock and disbelief. He was lucky to be unscathed. It was the sort of thing that might easily happen in a gale force wind. The air that day however was absolutely calm with barely a leaf stirring.

Manifestations of the spirit world were nothing new for me. Having grown up in the rambling Victorian house in Crystal Palace, with its doubtless rich history, I was well aware that people often stayed on in the places they had lived and probably died in. My dancers had been just that, taking the stage each night for me, as perhaps they had once trod the boards of some nearby theatre, in the gilded days of music hall. Here in this house though there lay something very different, a dark mystery surrounding the lonely figure of the boy, whose unhappy, unquiet spirit continued to scream his distress with angry doorbells and breaking glass.

We had been in the house about two and a half years when I fell pregnant. The psychic phenomena had not ceased, and I could still feel the eerie presence of the boy at all times. Knowing I would soon have a little one of my own, I realised this disturbed spirit could have adverse, potentially serious consequences. Concerned for the well being of our child in the malignant energy of the house, Mal agreed we had to move.

Being still signed up to the RAF, the options were limited, and as my time to give birth drew closer I became increasingly anxious. I was nearly eight months pregnant, when the chance of a posting to RAF Northolt came up, and with a feeling of relief we were able to leave the haunted house in Norfolk behind.

The birth was a traumatic one, but resulted in a beautiful baby boy, for whom we chose the name Neil. Shortly afterwards I went back to visit one of our former neighbours, a lady whom I had become friends with while in West Raynham. I mentioned my impressions of the house, and how I had seen and felt the strong presence of a spirit. The neighbour, who had been there many years, told me about a five-year-old boy who had once lived in the house. What happened to him? I asked. All she would say was that he had died there in tragic circumstances.

I had seen little of my sister Linda since marrying and moving away. We were in touch by phone though, and I knew that lately she and her husband had been going through a difficult patch. He was out of work, and with house prices beyond their means, they had been living with my mum. It was hardly an ideal situation, especially with Mum still drinking as seriously as ever. Finally things came to a head, and in 1981 Linda and her husband split up. This would have been hard enough at the best of times, but Linda also discovered she was pregnant.

After the birth she travelled up to Northolt, along with her baby, to stay with Mal and I and our own little one, now eighteen months old, in the RAF accommodation. I really bonded with Linda's lad, and loved him like my own. Linda herself just wasn't very maternal. After six weeks, the Air Force put an end to the sharing arrangement, and Linda and her baby had to move. Fortunately she found a hostel close by, where I was able to visit them every day. Shortly after that she was offered a flat, but in a part of London miles from Northolt. With neither of us able to drive, I would have to rely on Mal to take me over there, which for practical reasons couldn't be very often. I had got used to having Linda and her baby being close by, part of the family, now all too soon they were gone, and I missed them both terribly.

Premonitions continued to come to me. Some were frighteningly accurate. One morning over breakfast, I told Mal I had seen him driving near a bridge and a woman had stepped into the path of his car. When he returned later he told me it had happened, by a bridge a woman had walked out suddenly in front of him, forcing him to swerve and narrowly miss her. This might have been simply a sign to take care on the roads, or have meant something more, I didn't know. Something that couldn't be mistaken when they appeared however, were the signs telling me I was pregnant again.

Sixteen

It was 1983. My son Neil was three years old, and I was pleased as punch at the thought of a little brother or sister for him. I was also scared. Remembering the trauma of the first time, the experience of childbirth was not something I looked forward to. Mal had other misgivings; his concerned being that we could not afford another child. I strongly objected to this, and told him that to say such things was like cursing his child. This led to frequent arguments.

There seemed to be a cloud hanging over what should have been a happily expected event. What was more, despite no particular physical evidence, as the due date approached I got the distinct feeling that there was actually something wrong with the baby. A friend of mine was also expecting at the time, and when I confided in her about my anxieties she suggested I make an appointment with my doctor. Though I had no way of knowing then, I told the doctor I was convinced the child was a girl, and furthermore that things weren't right. The doctor more or less told me not to be silly, that there was nothing to worry about and the baby was fine. This should have put my mind at rest, but something was telling me otherwise.

Two days later I started having labour pains. I rang the surgery again, and this time a very nice lady doctor came out to see me. She said she wouldn't examine me, and that I should just rest. That night my waters broke, and I was rushed to hospital. The baby however was already dead. A post mortem was carried out but it wasn't till eight weeks later that I was given the results. This put the time of death at two days prior to my going to the hospital, in other words the day I had gone to see my doctor and told him there was something wrong. I was also told my baby had been a little girl. They said she had come away from the placenta.

I blamed myself for what had happened. I had known deep down that something was wrong, and now felt I should have tried harder to convince the doctors while there was still time to save the baby. If only I had sought help earlier, or got a second opinion. I should have been more insistent, stuck to my guns and made a nuisance of myself till someone listened, not allowed them to fob me off.

Now it was too late, a little baby girl had died, and try as I might I just couldn't shake off the overwhelming feelings of guilt and grief for her. I could see no light at the end of the tunnel. Increasingly depressed, and not eating or sleeping well, one day I got on the scales and saw that my weight had dropped to 6lbs 3ozs.

Time is a healer they say, but is rarely enough on it's own. After losing my baby and the subsequent depression, I underwent some counselling. Within a year or so, I was outwardly in better shape, able to function. The same could not be said for our marriage, which by this time was beginning to show signs of strain. I had taken a job in sales promotions, which though quite well paid, meant spending increasing amounts of time on the road and away from home, which I found hard to adjust to. With our financial commitments though, it wasn't so easy to walk away and find something else. I felt I was on a treadmill, where everything revolved around money and left little time for living.

Many couples though were in the same situation of having to juggle their lives. Money worries weren't the only reason our marriage was foundering. The loss of the baby probably hadn't helped. The old saying, 'marry in haste, repent in leisure' had also begun to echo. Getting hitched after knowing each other just three months, yes, we had been a bit hasty. I had been in a desperate situation at the time, Mal had wanted to help, and what's more we liked each other. People have exchanged vows for far worse reasons.

Then, out of the blue an unusual opportunity came up. Through the promotional job I'd been doing, someone wanted to play a part in a film. It seemed a genuine offer, and I was sent all the details of the movie and the shooting dates. The only snag was it meant spending a year in America. Mal was all for me going, but I couldn't bear the thought of being away from my little boy all that time.

Our relationship deteriorated still further, till eventually Mal and I agreed it would be better for us to part amicably. Perhaps we would be better friends than husband and wife. And so it was that in 1986, my son Neil and I went off to live in the Medway Towns.

Events meanwhile had not been standing still for other members of the family. My sister Linda had a new man in her life. Having fallen in love they had married, and now had a child together, a little girl.

I was pleased Linda had met someone and found some happiness again. Furthermore, since she now lived in Broadstairs, and I could now drive, we were only an hour apart, and so could meet up much more frequently. We also began phoning each other every night, and by 10.30pm, regular as clockwork, either she would call me, or I her, and we would chat for ages. When one door closes, another often opens, and for me this had meant Linda, and the renewal of our friendship.

One subject that frequently kept Linda and I talking on the phone was our mother. Having also remarried, Mum was now going through a difficult divorce. Still a heavy drinker, she had lately got into the habit of ringing up for no reason and shouting abuse down the phone at me. It was upsetting, and hard to know how to respond to her outbursts.

Linda and I being very close it perhaps wasn't surprising that what was now significant in her life, in other words her husband, should appear one day in one of my dreams. The nature of the dream however, was far from pleasant. As with Mal, it began with a vision of Linda's husband driving innocently along a road somewhere. Then I felt a sudden stab of alarm as something else entered the picture. This time the danger was not in human form, but a massive articulated lorry that had lurched across the road. As my brother-in-law braked frantically, his car went into a skid and disappeared beneath the huge wheels of the juggernaut.

Snapping out of the dream I desperately tried to get Linda on the phone.

'Is H OK?' I said immediately I got through 'Yes, why?' she replied. 'I saw his car go under a lorry.' Linda assured me her husband was all right.

After putting the phone down I didn't know what to do. Even if Linda had brushed off what I told her she would obviously be worrying right now. Was it wise to have called her I wondered? Thirty minutes after our conversation the police were at Linda's door; her husband had had an accident, his car had collided with a lorry. Fortunately, and miraculously, he was unscathed.

Why I had had the premonition was a mystery, clearly I hadn't been able to stop the event. Perhaps its meaning wasn't straightforward. Dreams can sometimes be symbolic, coded warnings of things to come.

Looking back, there was perhaps a connection with something about to occur in my own life. Though I did not know it, the cards were being dealt, and mine was going to be a knockout hand, in more ways than one.

Seventeen

It was in 1987 that I went to the doctor for a routine check up. After being examined, I was informed that they wanted to run some further tests. What kind of tests I wanted to know? The doctor then told me some pre-cancerous cells had been found near my womb, and advised that a biopsy must be arranged without delay.

Anyone who has been on the receiving end of this kind of news knows what it can do to you. However hard you try not to worry, there's this horrible, sick feeling in the pit of your stomach. All sorts of thoughts about life and death flash through your mind at a hundred miles an hour, and sleeping isn't easy. After the biopsy I was told the results would be known in ten days. This was to look for the presence of actual cancer, either around or in my womb.

Waiting is always the worst, the uncertainty chewing away at your nerve endings. The ten days seemed an eternity. When the results did come back, they showed that nothing malignant had as yet penetrated my womb. I thanked God. This didn't mean I was in the clear though. Treatment would be needed to remove the pre-cancerous tissue, and I would then have to return for regular checks for the next near, to make sure nothing else had started growing that shouldn't.

Another New Year came around, bringing in January among other things worrying news about Terry Waite, the Archbishop of Canterbury's special peace envoy to the Middle East. Having gone to Lebanon to plead for the release of hostages, he had now disappeared and was thought likely to haven been taken prisoner himself. Around the world, people were now praying for him.

In February I took a trip up to London, and having spent the day and evening there, it was gone midnight before I got on the M26 for the return journey home. I was used to driving longish distances now, and with the roads likely to be clearer it seemed perfectly reasonable to travel at night. This particular night however, the weather was freezing, and my hands shivered as they gripped the steering wheel. I turned the heater full up, and was soon feeling the benefit.

From the combination of a long, tiring day, and now the warmth in the car, I was also starting to get a bit drowsy. With only a few miles to go though, I pressed on, my body stiff with fatigue, my eyes staring fixedly at the road ahead. My eyelids were now growing very heavy, drooping down. I thought: if I just let them close for a brief second, it'll be fine. I did.

When I opened them again, the central reservation was coming towards me. The next instant there was a massive bang, and I felt my whole body being forced forward. Lights and shapes of vehicles, wheels screaming, flashed chaotically as the car, bouncing off the central barrier span sideways across the motorway. There was another bang, and with a tremendous jolt the black letters of a 'Maidstone' sign came hurtling up. With yet another bang, the car seemed to overbalance, and I had a sense of falling.

When the car had stopped I looked out. Everything was at a funny angle, and things lay scattered across the bonnet. I realised they were bits of the engine. Steam was hissing somewhere, and there was a smell of burning. I thought: 'I have to get out', then everything went black.

Eighteen

I was on my hands and knees. Beneath me was grass. I tried to get up but couldn't. Beside the grass was the hard shoulder. The motorway, which had been busy while I was driving, was now quiet. What had happened, and how long had I been here like this?

I felt something warm running from my forehead and down my cheek, and realised it was blood. This is it, I thought, I am going to die now. Then an agonising pain hit me in the head. In the distance I saw headlights, of what looked like a lorry. Still unable to stand I tried to unbend my body and shout: 'Help – please, help me.' Waving my hands, the effort sent pain shooting through my skull. The headlights were still coming. The lorry hadn't seen me. But when I looked again I saw the lights had halted. It had pulled over, and someone was running towards me.

The driver helped me along the icy hard shoulder then got me up into his cab where it was warm. There was a young lad in there. I heard him say it was his son. Then he was on the phone. In a while the police arrived, then an ambulance. The police told the lorry driver he could go. As I was put into the ambulance they gave me a warning about not getting into strangers' vehicles. At the hospital the doctors found I had a fractured skull, internal bleeding in my ears and bruising to my torso, legs and feet.

It was about four weeks before I could move around again. As my bodily injuries began to heal, my mind still had only a hazy knowledge of what had caused them. I kept trying to piece the events together; I knew I had hit the signpost and skidded off the road, but had no memory of the period between the car coming to a standstill and my crawling about on the grass verge. How much time had elapsed in between? When I asked about my car I was told it had been a write off. I felt a strong urge to see it.

At the breakers yard, the manager told me they were awaiting the insurers' assessment. There was a curious look on his face when I told him I had been driving the vehicle. 'You got out of that?' he said incredulously, and pointed to a jumble of metal in the corner. When he confirmed the registration I nodded. 'Well,' he said, 'all I can say is, that's what's called dicing with the devil and coming up trumps!' I could see the reason for his disbelief. The mangled car was unrecognisable.

How had I survived? There was of course the lorry driver; the stranger and my Good Samaritan, who had without a doubt saved my life. But how had I freed myself from the car prior to that? I couldn't help thinking of my dad, another lorry driver, a gentleman of the highway. To pull over and help was just the sort of thing he would have done for anyone. Had he somehow got me out of the car then called on another close father and child, out on the road together as we used to be, to rescue me on that cold, fateful night?

Dad knows my thoughts. As for the unknown trucker, whom I never got the chance to thank and whose name I never knew – I will be eternally grateful to him.

Later that year the doctors gave me the all clear on the cancer scare. It was time to thank God again.

Nineteen

In 1996 I received some unexpected news. My mum had got married again, this time without telling anyone. To be precise she had told my older sister, and she in turn had kept it to herself. That Mum had found someone to share her life with was to be welcomed, but why had she gone off and done it without even informing, let alone inviting Linda and I? Though used to Mum's ways, we couldn't help feeling hurt.

When more was known about her new husband however, it partly explained the secrecy. The fact he was from the Ukraine made no difference whatsoever; what was worrying was that like Mum, he appeared to be an alcoholic. From then on Mum did not like me to visit her if he was around, and when he was, the two of them would sit in the house and get drunk together.

One day my older sister picked up the phone and heard Mum's voice, tearful and distraught. Without any warning, her husband had dropped down dead. He and Mum had been married not much more than a year.

Mum was in deep shock, and as the months went by found it hard to cope. As she continued to drink heavily, and had a tendency not to eat properly, Linda and I travelled up from Kent to see her when we could. We would make her proper meals, and encourage her to do the same. My older sister still lived nearby and looked in on Mum fairly regularly, but with work and her own family to care for she obviously couldn't be there all the time. Linda and I made a point of calling Mum every day, asking if she was OK, checking she was eating, and urging her to cut down the drink and cigarettes.

A year went by, and Mum's condition, her loss of weight and noticeable frailty had become an increasing cause for concern. She really did seem to be wasting away.

My own condition was also undergoing a change, though a happy one, since I was now expecting another child. Linda and I continued our regular phone calls to Mum, though these were no substitute for being close by, especially as she did not always pick up the receiver, and we had no way of knowing if she alright.

Unable to get answer on the phone one day, I went round to call on her. I rang the bell, knocked loudly on the door and called out several times, but there was still no reply. Going round the back of the house I managed to get the kitchen window open, and - at four months pregnant - climbed in. I found Mum curled up on the floor, sobbing and whimpering.

It was heartbreaking to see my mother in such a pitiful state. She was admitted to a psychiatric hospital in Warlingham, Surrey, where the doctor said she appeared to have had a number of mild strokes, which had given her in some ways the mind of child. She would still not eat, and I began going to the hospital every day to feed her.

During these visits she would sometimes call me names and throw her food at me. She also kept saying the nurses were trying to kill her and take her babies, murmuring, 'Michael, Michael...'

Michael, the child who had died so long ago in the dark days of the war - of all the infants she had lost, he had never been forgotten, for she had kept him alive in her heart all this time.

Whenever my mother threw her tantrums or was difficult, the hospital staff would comment on how I seemed to have so much more patience with her than they did. The fact was, she was my mum, and I loved her.

When my mother was ready to leave the hospital, the family discussed what to do next. Clearly she could not go back to her own home for she now needed close care and attention. A residential home, ideally one that would bring her closer to Linda and I, might be the answer. Moving would be a wrench for her, especially after thirty odd years in the same house and a lifetime in and around south London, but with her health now the main priority, it seemed on balance the best solution, assuming we could find somewhere suitable. After some investigations we located a place that felt right. It was situated on the Kent coast, and, crucially was only a half hour drive from where I lived, likewise about the same distance from Linda.

Reassured that she now had 24-hour care, living nearby I was able to call in and see Mum almost every day. We would walk together to the local shops, drive to the sea and have trips out for dinner. Although the care home was a new environment for Mum, there was a positive side to it. The set daily routine meant that she now had regular good meals, her smoking and drinking were curbed, and she was encouraged to have a little daily exercise combined with regular rest periods. She began to make friends too, helping to take her out of herself. Within a few weeks the benefits were showing, as Mum gained weight and began looking generally fitter and healthier.

I was to discover it wasn't only her physical condition that had altered. It happened quite out of the blue, one morning not long after she had moved to the home. We were sat together, just chatting, when she looked up at me and said, 'I used to hate you, I don't know why. But I do love you.'

Mum's words took me by surprise. In effect she was confessing, acknowledging how difficult things had been during much of my childhood, and how sorry she clearly now was. That had taken courage and honesty. I was so glad that our trips out lately, the shopping together, just our companionship was giving her some pleasure, a simple happiness. Most of all I felt deeply touched that after all these years she had opened her heart to me. In that same conversation she mentioned again the lost little boy she had cherished, only this time not in fear, but hope. With a faraway look in her eyes, she said, 'I'll see my Michael soon.' All I could say to her was, 'Yes Mum, one day you will.'

Shortly afterwards I had a dream about my mother. She was lying in bed with her arms at her sides, when two figures, both male, appeared. They each took gentle hold of her outstretched arms, lifting her out of the bed, and up, up, up.

Twenty

Those who have gone to spirit are never entirely departed, and every so often will find a complete stranger to make their presence felt. In the year 2000 I happened to be one of those strangers.

By now my daughter Amelia was three years old, and I had another baby girl, Shania. Together with my sons David, and Neil the oldest at twenty-one, the five of us were in need of somewhere to live. Having been offered a council house in Gillingham I went round to take a look. Peering up at the windows I had an uneasy feeling about the place. Beggars couldn't be choosers however, and I agreed to take it.

The first night in the house was like a flashback to West Raynham, for here too, someone was watching. Waking up and thinking it morning, I checked my watch to find it was only 2 a.m. Light was flooding in to the bedroom from the bulb on the landing. I knew for a fact I had turned everything off when I went to bed. Assuming my son had got up in the night and left the landing light on, I switched it off and went back to sleep.

The following night it happened again. Neil was adamant he hadn't left any lights on. I examined the switch and bulb socket but they both looked in order. Sure enough the same thing occurred on the third night, and the night after, and on it went, always around the same time, 2 a.m. As well as the light, some nights there was a noise, a gentle tinkling sound from somewhere in the house, like an old-fashioned musical box.

The next manifestation came during the day. I was on the ground floor when I saw a figure, that of a tall man, go running up our stairs. At first I thought it was an actual person, and shouted up to my son, unsure if it was someone he knew or an intruder. Neil came to the top of the stairs and said he had not seen, or heard anyone.

Many times during the night I was conscious of a presence, like someone was on the bed. I was a single mum now, my baby slept in her cot, and there was no one else who could be in the room, but nonetheless I could feel this distinct weight. Then one night getting up for a pee, I made my way towards the bathroom and, as I took hold of the door handle it tugged against me. Thinking my son was in there I called out 'Sorry', let go of the handle and stepped away. The door then swung ajar, and the bathroom appeared to be empty. I say appeared, for my heart was now racing. I knew this was the spirit male I had seen running up the stairs.

Another spirit also lived in the house. This was an elderly female, a kindly old soul whom I would often talk to in the kitchen. One evening my little girl came to me sobbing, saying 'nanny is laying on the floor upstairs with blood coming out of her mouth.' I comforted her and told her it was a silly dream. It was a terrible image for a child to have dreamt, but privately I wondered about the kindly old soul, and whether there was a story there.

There was, and it was about to unfold in a frightening fashion. It began with my son, angry and upset, confronting me one morning, 'Who did you have here last night?' he demanded.

'Neil', no one's been here,' I said.

'Then who was that bloke calling me a lazy sod, and telling me to get up and help my mother?' said Neil.

'What on earth do you mean love?' I said. Then as he turned slightly I noticed something on his body, a pattern of welts across his back, the skin red raw as if he had been whipped or beaten. I knew at once the male spirit had attacked him in the night. Horrified, I spoke to the spirit, telling him he didn't frighten us, and to go, leave us alone.

A couple of days later I had a chat with our neighbour. She told me of an old lady who had died in our house, and whose decomposing body had only been discovered three months later. The whole place had had to be fumigated. A year before her death, the old lady's only son had committed suicide. Neither of these poor souls could rest, and whilst the old lady remained benign, the spirit of her tragic son continued to exude malevolence, especially towards my son.

Not for the first time, I found myself entangled with a stubborn and destructive spirit. As before, the only course of action was to leave the spirit be, let whatever diabolical energy was tormenting it burn itself out alone. My children and I found alternative accommodation, and closed the door for the last time on this unhappy house.

Twenty-One

It was in June of 2001, that I awoke in the early hours of the morning with severe chest pains. My first thought was that something was wrong with Mum. I immediately telephoned the care home, but getting no reply called my older sister and asked if she had been contacted about Mum. She assured me she had heard nothing. I continued calling the home throughout the night, and finally at 6 a.m., someone answered.

'Is my mother all right?' I asked. I was told that a doctor had been called in to Mum during the night, and would be returning shortly to do an ECG. I put the phone down and set off for the home. When I arrived I went in and sat with Mum till the ECG results were known. They confirmed that she had suffered a heart attack in the night. Without doubt spirit had let me know.

By way of a change for Mum, and to show her the old neighbourhood again, we would sometimes pick her up then go back to my older sister's house in New Addington to spend the day together there. One morning in September 2001, arriving at the care home to collect her as arranged, we found her sat in the entrance lobby with some of the other ladies. Seeing us Mum got up and said cheerio to her friends. As she did so, one of them called her back.

'Ellen!' she said, 'You forgot your shoes and coat.' Looking down we saw Mum had no shoes on.

Mum however just smiled and replied, 'I don't need them dear. I won't be coming back.' We all laughed, Mum included. She then went and fetched her shoes and coat, said goodbye to her friends again, and off we went to New Addington.

We had been at my older sister's a couple of hours, Linda wasn't with us, and the rest of us were having a cup of tea and had just put on the television, when Mum said she needed to use the bathroom. Although a little frail and slow, she liked to manage the stairs on her own, and so off she went.

Drinking our tea, we began flipping round the TV channels to see what was on. One programme that caught our attention looked like a preview for a new film, one of those disaster movies. One scene kept repeating: an aeroplane appeared to lose control and collide with a tall building; then there came smoke, people running, panic.

Suddenly we realised; this was no film but reality. The buildings were the twin towers of the world trade centre in New York, and the aeroplanes had been flown deliberately into them. The people inside the buildings were trapped, the fires slowly creeping up to engulf them, the two massive structures already weakened and buckling in the intense heat. All the main channels were showing the same story; the whole world transfixed in horror at what they were witnessing. It was so appalling it beggared belief.

Engrossed in what was unfolding on the TV, we had momentarily forgotten Mum was still upstairs. Then for some reason I turned from the screen and said to my older sister, 'Something's the matter with Mum – turn the TV down, quick.'

It was then we heard a very faint cry from above. We both rushed upstairs and could hear Mum saying, 'Help, help,' ever so softly.

'Mum!' I called, running to the bathroom. I tried the handle, which fortunately didn't seem to be locked. When I attempted to go in however I could only get the door open a couple of inches. Something was in the way. Peering through the narrow opening between the door and the frame, I saw the pattern of Mum's clothes. She must have collapsed, and was lying across the door unable to move.

My older sister immediately ran back downstairs to phone for an ambulance. Meanwhile, for all we knew Mum may have stopped breathing, and we had to try to get in to her. I slid my hand and wrist into the gap in the door, and tried to squeeze the rest of my arm through. If I could make it a little further I would be able to reach her. I heard her voice speaking faintly again.

'Hold on Mum,' I called back, 'soon have you out.' Then I realised she wasn't talking to me. 'Not yet George,' she said, 'not yet, I'm not ready.' George was my dad - Mum was talking to him in spirit. Desperate now to reach her, I pushed my arm hard into the gap, the doorframe scraping my skin. By groping around I managed to take hold of Mum's clothes. With an effort I tried to tug her to one side, but it was no good. At the angle I was at, and using only one arm I simply hadn't the strength or leverage to move her. I prayed the ambulance would come soon.

While resting for a split second to catch my breath, on the other side of the door, I felt a touch on my skin. The touch then became someone's hand, holding my forearm. Mum must have taken my arm, and was pulling on it to move herself clear of the door. I gripped her clothes and heaved once more. Now she was moving. It seemed miraculous, but she had partly levered herself out of the way. I would never have thought she had such strength at the best of times. In another second the door swung open and my older sister and I were able to enter the room.

Even as I knelt down to Mum to check her condition, something odd struck me; she was lying on her front, her two arms tucked completely beneath her body. How then could she have taken my forearm, let alone lifted herself across the floor?

My older sister's family were on the scene now, and together we carried Mum carefully into the bedroom. Laying her down on the bed, she curled into the foetal position. I lay down with her and tried to cuddle her, but though breathing her body felt cold and clammy, and her skin had a grey pallor. I found a shawl and wrapped her in it.

She then spoke again: 'I've got to go now, got to go,' she said.

'Mum,' I said to her, 'please don't worry, the ambulance is on its way, it won't be long now, really – hold on.'

All she would say was, 'It's too late, too late.'

A few minutes later the ambulance arrived. The paramedics came upstairs and put Mum onto a stretcher, reassuring her all the while. Once in the ambulance, she was wired up to a monitor checking her pulse, respiration and body temperature. I was given a fold down seat beside her in the back, from where I could hold her hand. Two of the medics sat in with us, the doors were closed and we were off.

We had gone probably less than a mile when Mum turned her head to me. Her eyes were open and her pupils looked dilated. Suddenly I gasped for air, as if all the breath had been taken from my body. At the same moment I felt Mum's soul pass through me. I said, 'She is gone now.'

The medics at once sprang into action, administering oxygen and cardiac massage. Despite all attempts to resuscitate her, by the time we reached the hospital Mum was dead.

I was devastated, numb with shock. I thought of my Linda, who didn't know yet. When I rang her and broke the news we both cried for a long time, two sisters together in grief. Nothing would be the same now our Mum had gone, not ever again.

The next morning the papers were full of what had happened in America, the awful events we had watched while Mum was upstairs, during the last hour of her life. It had been the last hour for so many others, the thousands of people now known to have been at work in the twin towers when the planes hit. Overnight the whole world seemed to have turned to darkness.

I thought again of the uncanny way either Mum or I had suddenly found such strength to lift her, and of what I had heard her saying through the bathroom door. From the way she had talked to Dad, his spirit must have been present in the house. Was it he who had taken my arm and, knowing her time was near, helped me to reach her, so I could be with her in those final precious minutes? I felt sure he had known, and was preparing to be with Mum himself once again, and all the lost children too.

A few days later I was back at my own home and sat in the living room, quite alone in the house, when I got a sense of someone touching my neck and moving my hair. The feeling intensified for a few seconds then went away. Opposite me in the room was a rather pretty arrangement of dried flowers, a gift to Mum from one of her friends, which on an impulse I had brought home with me. Gazing at the flowers I felt a strong urge to take a photograph of them.

Later on I put the photo on the computer, and as the image came up on the screen I saw something peculiar. Beside the flowers was a white outline, the figure of a lady. After examining it more closely, I sent it to Linda, who immediately phoned me. 'That's Mum,' she said, 'you know she loved flowers.'

This was true, and that day she had been there with me in the room, giving my hair an affectionate stroke, something that had seldom happened during my childhood. But then a lot had changed in the last few years of her life. Mum had mellowed, and we had come to love one another. With the help of my dad, I had been able to be with her as she passed to spirit, and now both Linda and I felt she was with us.

Mum's funeral took place about a fortnight later. At the graveside I stood with my sisters and the rest of the family as the coffin was laid to rest in the earth. When the vicar's recitation from the Bible, and the traditional throwing on of earth and flowers had been performed, we stood for a while in respectful silence, contemplating the departed and the solemnity of the occasion.

Next to me was my older sister, and beside her, her granddaughter Danielle. As the other mourners drifted away, I turned to my sister and said quietly, 'Danielle's pregnant'.

Danielle, overhearing me, said immediately, 'No I'm not!' Certainly she showed no sign she was carrying.

A little while afterwards however, my older sister phoned me and confirmed Danielle was indeed going to have a baby. At the time of the funeral she would have been only about two weeks gone. Only spirit would have known.

Twenty-Two

After the passing of our mum, Linda and I became even closer. She would often phone and ask if Mum had 'visited' me. When I regretfully replied no, we would go on to talk about other things, usually at great length, our conversations often lasting an hour or more. With me still living in the Medway Towns, and Linda in Broadstairs we couldn't meet up as often as we'd like, so when a council house became available in Whitstable, I decided to move. Hopefully we could then spend more time together, and less money on our phone bills!

Linda, or Lou as I had called her since childhood, had changed so much. She still took life very much as it came, but no longer felt the need to take on the whole world. Gone at last were the days of giving someone a verbal bashing to prove a point, or even a black eye. Now she was much more easy going, a homely mum, and devoted to her kids.

Linda's new, positive outlook on life showed in her love of exercise, especially swimming, and the pleasures of nature. Perhaps picking up some tricks from Dad, she had transformed her modest back garden into a place of beauty, and could name every flower, herb and bush. She was also a brilliant cook, and loved having people round for dinner.

After my move to Whitstable Linda and I began seeing each other regularly – a bit of shopping, a bite to eat, or just a chat. It was easy going and so nice, just like the old days when we had both just started out at work. My Lou had mellowed. I had got her back, and we were friends again the way sisters should be.

In settling down though Linda had lost neither her outgoing nature nor, as I was to discover, her ability to charm people, friends and strangers alike. One weekend, she invited me over to a pub called The Albion in Broadstairs. The attraction here was live entertainment, which included karaoke, and Linda, having always been a bit of performer herself was naturally drawn to the ambience.

Now karaoke nights, as those that have experienced them will know, are not so much about having a great voice, as having a great time. Sometimes the most entertaining singers are the awful ones and the drunks, whose sheer pizzazz earns them a good-natured clap. Linda though wasn't in that category. At the Albion, when it was her turn to sing, she chose the Patsy Cline song "Crazy". I had always thought Linda had a lovely voice, and that night she proved it. The audience loved her, and cheered for more.

The Albion became a regular destination for us on a Friday. There was usually a good crowd in; Linda would sing "Crazy" or some other favourite songs, have a few drinks and socialise. She was actually very flirtatious, but in a funny way, and could have people in stitches sometimes, me included.

Life wasn't all a bed of roses though. Linda's medical history was unusual, having had an early menopause at the age of thirty-one, and for some time since she had experienced chronic back pain. This was a common enough complaint, but for my sister so severe some days it made it hard for her to stay upright. I remembered how on the day of Mum's funeral she had found it hard going, what with all the standing. What was causing the problem? After a few visits to the doctor, the diagnosis had come back that she was suffering from osteoporosis.

Linda had never been one to take things lying down. Undaunted by the increasing difficulty of getting around, she took on the role of events secretary at the Albion, booking in the bands and arranging the entertainment. Employing her excellent culinary skills, she also provided the bar food and catering for parties and functions in the pub. And whenever it was a karaoke night, she'd be up there singing her heart out.

One day Linda woke to find she couldn't get out of bed. Over the next few months her physical condition continued to decline, and soon she was unable to walk without help. Nothing was gong to stop her going out however, especially to the Albion, even this meant in a wheelchair, and eventually that's what it had to be. With either me or someone else to get her there, she carried on her duties as entertainments secretary, caterer, vocalist, and generally being the life and soul of the party.

In what seemed a relatively short space of time, Linda had become an invalid. And although her spirit remained outwardly strong, I was now increasingly concerned about her mental health. Having previously had a tendency towards depression, the pain and frustration of her new situation often plunged her into dark, melancholy moods. On many occasions she told me she did not want to live, that she wanted to be with Mum and Dad. This made me very afraid. When I mentioned these remarks to her partner during a phone conversation, he shrugged it off, assuring me Linda was fine.

Then one night I had a dream, very specific, and vivid in its detail. In it I found myself in church, seated next to my older sister. 'Where's Linda?' I asked. My sister pointed to a coffin by the altar. Then a voice said to me, 'Do you have any words for her?' and saw on my right a vicar. I then woke up with a start and cried. When I called my older sister, she told me to dismiss it, it was a dream, nothing more. She also told me not to say anything about it to Linda.

It was Christmas 2002, and for the big day, Linda had invited my children and I down to her house in Broadstairs. We arrived after dinner as planned, expecting just to have a play and a chat and exchange the traditional gifts. When we had all sat down however, Linda, with a flourish, produced three large, bulging bin liners. 'What on earth have you got in there, Lou?' I said. When the children were invited to take a look, they found the bags stuffed full of presents of all shapes and sizes.

'Happy Christmas!' she announced, handing over the bags

'Say thank you to Auntie Linda children.' I called above the whoops of delight.

As the excited youngsters tore open the goodies, covering the floor in a mountain of paper, I quietly chided Linda for spending so much money, which I knew she couldn't really afford. Smiling, she replied, 'I wanted to give the kids a Christmas they wouldn't forget.'

In April 2003, one Thursday night, the phone rang. It was Linda. It was my birthday the following day, and she wanted me to come out with her and celebrate. Being on my own and unable to get a babysitter for the evening, I had to say no.

On the Saturday morning I had another phone call. It was to inform me that at 2.30am the previous night, Linda's partner had found her in bed unconscious and having difficulty breathing, and that she had been rushed to hospital. It was thought she had inhaled her own vomit.

When I arrived at the hospital Linda was in intensive care. She remained unconscious throughout the night and all the following day. I remained by her bed, watching her face intently for some sign, the slightest flicker of movement. Eventually I went away and slept for a bit.

The next day I asked Mal if he could mind the children while I visited the hospital. He accepted, but was grudging about it. He seemed unable to understand why I wanted to go, it was not my responsibility, was his attitude. I felt completely alone.

When I returned to the hospital there was still no change. The monitors Linda was wired up to showed her pulse steady, her respiration regular. I sat by her side the next day, and the day after and the day after that, sleeping only when tiredness overcame me. For long periods I held her hand, sometimes talking to her, of ordinary, trivial things, and reassuring her, discussing what we would do when she came home.

All the while the screen showed the rising line of her heartbeat, like the waves made in a skipping rope when you shake it. 'Salt mustard, vinegar, pepper.' Linda. Lou I still called her. Dad and me, it was our nickname for her when we were kids. 'Come on Lou…' I pictured us playing in the garden of the prefab, recalling the scene, pushing each other on the rickety swing and singing, Dad patiently tending his vegetable patch.

What Linda was attached to was a life support machine. After eleven days a doctor came and spoke to me. He said a decision had to be taken; there was nothing more they could do for her. It felt like the ground was opening up beneath me.

After consent had been given, I leaned over the bed, and taking her hand whispered softly, 'Linda, go to Mum and Dad – they're waiting for you.' When the machine was switched off I watched as the lines on the monitor slowed, each pulsation a little weaker than the last, the skipping rope falling, as the life gradually ebbed away. Ever since we were children I had wanted to protect my Linda, I could not bear to see her suffer. Now she was about to die. Soon would come the last beat of her heart. I turned my head away.

Not wishing to look on her lifeless body, I immediately busied myself gathering up her few belongings, tears rolling down my cheeks. As I did so I heard someone say: 'Tina.' I looked around but no one was there. Then a nurse opened the door. 'Did a man just come in here?' I asked. 'No,' replied the nurse, 'no one has come in.' Had it been Dad's voice calling me, letting me know that our Lou was safe in his arms?

I left the hospital and went back to an empty house. Mal was looking after the kids. Alone now, the awful reality of what had happened hit me with renewed force. My Linda had gone, my loving sister who I had grown up with and shared so many memories. I would never see her again. Oh Lou…!

In a violent storm of grief I threw myself on the floor screaming, 'No, not my Linda, no, oh God why, why, why…?' Not knowing what I was doing I went out and jumped in the car. I drove off and put my foot down hard, going at breakneck speed, praying that God would take me. It was then I thought of my children, and how they needed me. I slowed the car and returned home.

The day before Linda's funeral I went to the undertakers to see her one last time. 'You look beautiful,' I said. On a chair was her make-up. Knowing she would like to have a little on, I carefully applied some lipstick and eye shadow to her face, talking to her as I worked. When I had finished I took her cold hand in mine. I said: 'Wait for me,' then I kissed her and left.

Leaving the funeral parlour, I went up to the seafront. There was not a soul in sight, the air bracing. I walked along a little way, and passing a public convenience stopped to pay a visit. As I crossed the grass verge, I heard someone call my name: 'Tina.' It was the same voice, the one that had spoken to me at Linda's bedside at the moment of her passing. 'Dad?' A strange feeling came over me. I was being given a sign, shown a direction. In that instant, out of my utter desolation at the loss of Linda, there came a sense that my role on the earthly plane was about to begin.

At Linda's funeral the church was packed, not only with family, but lots of people from the Albion. Many spoke of her as a vibrant soul, who touched their lives with her humour, her warmth, and her love. Linda as I well knew, would be anyone's friend, would give anyone a hug or a cuddle, a kind word.

The vicar came and spoke to me, just as in my dream, using the exact same phrase: 'Do you have any words for her?' I told him yes, and when the time came read out the words I had composed for my darling sister.

'My Lou, I'm so glad you were my sister and my closest friend.

I will miss our chats, your laughter and your great sense of humour.

I will miss your little turned up nose, and your crazy ways as we were growing up.

My Lou I will miss our evening calls; the phone doesn't ring anymore, but we will see each other again, and when we do, there will be so much for us to catch up on.

God needed an Angel and he chose you. I love you Lou, more than anything, and life is going to be tough without you, but you will always remain in my heart,

God Bless You Sweetheart. Your loving sister Tina xxx'
25-06-1958 - 16-04-2003

Twenty-Three

After the funeral there was still the mystery of precisely what had happened the night Linda was rushed to hospital. The exact circumstances were unclear. An inquest had been held, which four weeks later delivered the verdict that her death had been accidental.

What did this amount to? It confirmed that no one else was to blame, but gave no clue as to Linda's own intentions and state of mind in her last hours of consciousness. There was however one thing that had not been taken into account; the night Linda passed out she had left a note on her dressing table. Perhaps this had been a cry for help, or an attempt to deal with her feelings of despair. Whatever the motive, the outcome had been tragic, and the painful question remained: had Linda really meant to take her own life? Only she could tell us.

I kept thinking of the night she had called, eager to see me and go out, and I had turned her down for lack of a babysitter. It was the last time I heard her voice. Why had I not just taken the kids with me? If only I had done that one small thing, might she still be alive? The thought tormented me. If there was ever a time I would give anything to turn back the clock, this was it.

I was desperately upset following the inquest. Driving home later I found myself suddenly in floods of tears at the wheel, and the next thing I knew I had been pulled over by the police for speeding. Apparently I had been doing a hundred and four miles an hour. I told the officers about my sister and the inquest, and how it had affected me, but they said this was no excuse.

Afterwards I phoned my son Neil, who was staying with Mal. When Mal answered the phone, and I told him about the speeding incident, he had a real go at me, and said, 'Won't you ever learn!' But it had been the same the whole way through - leaving the hospital after visiting Linda, he would say to me, 'Don't show the kids you're upset, don't cry, just get in the car.' He couldn't even see why I had wanted to go there every day.

Linda and I had been like one. My older sister had her own family, and Mum and Dad were both gone. Linda and I were so special to each other, part of each other, going right back to our childhood. She

92

could never be replaced, and no one seemed to understand that. Mal's indifference was all part of the cold, unfeeling world that now seemed to engulf me. No one was there for me. I grieved alone.

About a month later I was sitting in my dining room, when I felt something warm gripping my right arm. Immediately I said, 'Linda, is that you?' The sensation went away. I said, 'If that's you Lou, please do that again, touch my arm.' Again I felt the warm grip. Tears streaming down my face, I knew that Linda had visited me.

That night, before going to bed I took a pen and paper and set them out on the table. I then locked the door to the dining room and went upstairs. As I got into bed I thought: what a silly fool I am.

Nevertheless I couldn't sleep. Thoughts kept running through my head, and all the while I felt an overwhelming urge to return to the dining room and see if anything had happened to the pen and paper. When it got to 5 a.m. I couldn't stand it any longer. I went downstairs, unlocked the dining room and went in. There on the table was the paper as I had left it, still a blank page. My heart sank. Had I really expected Linda to write me a message in the night? Disappointed, I turned to go back to bed.

Then I realised something wasn't quite right. The pen I had left out was not on the paper; in fact it wasn't anywhere on the table. Looking down I saw it on the carpet. Assuming it must have rolled off, I picked it up and dropped it back on the table. I noticed however that it didn't move when it landed. I picked it up again and repeated the experiment a few times. Always it stayed put where it fell. I then tilted the table from various angles, but the pen remained in place. Whatever I did I could not make the pen roll out of place. There was no window open in the room and no draughts, neither did I have a cat or dog that could have disturbed the table, and in any case the door had been locked since I left it. The only way the pen would move was to push it directly or pick it up. Had Lou done that, had she tried to leave me a message? I wanted to believe so.

Still grieving and missing Lou terribly, I threw all my energies into my children. Neil and his younger brother David were both autistic. Neil, now twenty-three was still living at home with me and not working, as his condition made him unsettled about going out. Meanwhile David was being bullied at school, and I was desperately trying to sort out appropriate education for him. With the two girls Amelia and Shania as well, life for us in a three-bedroom house on the rather rough Grimes Hill estate in Whitstable, was not easy. In fact I was at my wit's end trying to cope, and as the practical and emotional difficulties spiralled, I approached the council for help. They said there was a possibility of re-housing, but as always, a waiting list.

Several months went by, until, a year after my sister's passing, the council contacted us. I was notified that a house had become vacant in Herne Bay, and we could move in shortly. Thank god was all I could say.

It was in May of 2004, while exploring the byways of Herne Bay, I came across a little sign saying 'Spiritualist Church.' I looked on the board for the date of the next meeting and decided to go along. Apart from the touch on my arm and the moving of the pen that night, I had as yet received no communication from Linda. Perhaps at such a gathering some message from her might just reach me.

There were quite a few people at the church when I arrived, but looking around I saw a vacant seat next to a middle-aged lady and an older gentleman. When everyone was settled, the medium for the evening stood up and came on to the platform. She turned her attention to a lady seated a couple of rows from me. As the medium spoke, I saw, beside the lady she was addressing, the figure of a boy. I turned to the lady next to me. 'Why isn't she mentioning the child?' I whispered. 'Child – what child?' my neighbour replied. 'The one sitting next to her,' I said. My neighbour peered over but obviously could not see any child. At that moment the medium announced: 'You have a child in spirit.' The lady concerned nodded. 'Yes,' she said, 'my son.' When the medium moved on to others in the room I saw more people in spirit and heard their thoughts, which would then be spoken by the medium. As the evening wore on I was receiving message after message, all of which were quickly confirmed.

Sadly I had received no message from Linda that night. But I knew now it was my turn to work for spirit. I wanted to communicate again, just as I had done with my spirit friends when I was a child. I could again hear such spirits, I could see them, but I didn't know how to channel the ability, or what to do next.

Then one evening, after I had attended a few more meetings, the church president announced that they would be starting what she called a beginners' circle, explained what this was, and invited anyone who was interested to join. Straightaway I put my name down. The day I had seen Linda for the last time, kissed her and said goodbye, then heard the voice by the seafront calling my name, had already told me what I must do. I was now about to be shown how.

Twenty-Four

One of the first exercises for the beginners' circle at the Spiritualist Church was the practice of meditation. For this we were asked to close our eyes for a set period of time, and tell the rest of the circle what images came into our minds. Most people saw colours or patterns of one sort or another. I however saw faces, lots of them and all in motion, travelling down a kind of tunnel. One face was that of a man, who came speeding straight at me, but as he got close I saw that half of his face was actually missing. Almost immediately I saw another image, of an aeroplane being shot down, screaming past out of control. Snapping out of the meditation I opened my eyes.

'Time's not up yet,' said the president, looking at me. 'Sorry,' I replied, 'but I saw a man.'

'No, no,' she said, 'you didn't follow me through the meditation, you weren't listening.' I told her I had tried, but that as soon as I closed my eyes I saw people. By now the president was getting quite upset that I wasn't following the proper procedure. The lady in the next seat then whispered to me. 'What did you see Christina?' I told her about the face with one half missing, and the shot out aeroplane. She gave a gasp. 'Oh my god, that was my brother!' she said. 'Please, please, did you get anything else?' At this point, overhearing our conversation, the president snapped,

'Christina - we're not here to give messages!' I said no more. I felt like a naughty child who had been told off

As I attended further meetings, I continued to receive messages about people, which more often than not I couldn't resist passing on. Four weeks after my first meeting, a visiting medium attended our circle. A friend of our church president, she had over twenty years experience, and ran circles herself. The president, who by now had had quite enough of my messages, took it as an opportunity to put me in my place. 'Right, she announced, 'if you have spirit with you, we're going to do a test.'

I was put into the circle with twenty people around me, and blindfolded quite tightly. I couldn't see a thing. The visiting medium then said, 'Christina, I'm going to put my hand over someone's head. They won't speak, only nod. I will speak for them by saying yes or no. You must bring a spirit through for them, and a message.' I had never done this before, having only received messages involuntarily. However I said, 'OK.'

All was silent around me as I waited, blinking in the darkness. Within a few seconds I could see a large lady with curly hair. Then I heard her voice. 'Thank you,' she said, 'for the red rose you laid on my grave today.' Repeating this aloud, I waited for a response from the visiting medium. 'Yes,' she said. Then more messages came to me, tumbling into my head one after another. Each time I repeated them the visiting medium gave a 'Yes'. When I had finished, the blindfold was taken off. I was no longer doubted.

A week later I was put into the advanced class. Held upstairs, this comprised professional, working mediums already serving at various churches. At the end of the first evening we all exchanged phone numbers. I began regular attendance at the class, and it was after one particular meeting, on the way home, that I felt the presence of a female spirit. She kept telling me her name was Doris Bovis, and I sensed she had a message for a man called Michael who was one of the mediums at the church. I rang him up and asked if the name Bovis meant anything to him. He was not altogether pleased. 'Don't go there,' he said, 'Bovis is my birth name.' He had been adopted, he said, and had always used his adoptive parents' surname. 'Oh I see,' I said, 'well anyway the message I have is from a Doris Bovis.' He replied that he didn't know any Doris, and that his birth mother's Christian name had been Mavis. Since he didn't want to pursue the matter I dismissed it.

I had been in the circle three months when I received a phone call from Michael. It had nothing to do with spirit messages though, at least that's how it appeared at first. Michael had rung to ask a favour. Due to attend a spiritualist event in Dover, his car had broken down and he desperately needed a lift. 'I don't know,' I replied, 'I'll have to see if I can get someone to look after the kids.' I spoke to my son Neil, who agreed to mind the young ones for the evening, and then phoned Michael back.

A little while later we arrived at Dover Spiritualist Church. As we came in, the president of the church, whose name was Fred, announced, 'It's our fledgling night, but the only thing is we're a medium short.' Then looking at me he said. 'Would you like to have a go?' I stared at him. 'Me?' I said. 'Yes, why not?'

I looked round at the people filing in and sitting down, already quite a few of them. I was used to receiving messages in the circle, among a supportive group of peers, but this was a public event, working on platform in front of an audience who would really be expecting something. It was all very well getting up there, but supposing I couldn't deliver? This was for professionals. I was an amateur, surely.

'Oh no,' I said, feeling quite flustered, 'I couldn't…' Then Michael, who was due to go up himself said, 'Go on, you can sit up on platform with me. If you don't get anything, don't worry.' Without further thinking I said, 'OK.'

As the proceedings commenced I went and took my place up on the platform. My heart was racing. The moment I stood up however, I could see spirits, I could hear them coming closer, eager to break through and communicate, speaking to me. From that point on there was no stopping; I gave message after message to all sorts of people in the room, one after another greeted with a yes, a yes, a yes.

Looking back, I saw the chain of events that led me to that first night on platform at Dover as something meant to be. A car breaking down, the missing medium, and then me, just happening to be on the spot; if these accidents hadn't coincided, I wondered if I would ever have had the courage to take that next step, to get up there and work in front of the public. But I didn't believe it was accidental. Spirit had a helping hand in putting me out there.

From then on, each week Michael allowed me to accompany him on the platform. I had the sense of having set forth on a journey, and as I gained in experience that my real work was beginning.

Perhaps it was also no coincidence that there were to be further developments in the riddle of Doris Bovis. It was in December of that year, again while I was coming home from church, that she revisited me. This time she had a request. I phoned Michael. 'Doris is back,' I told him, 'and she has a message for you – she needs you to find Tony.'

After a brief pause he replied, 'Tony? That's my brother - he was adopted too. But as I told you, I don't know any Doris.' Not having a copy of his birth certificate he was curious about the matter, and that same week sent off for it. When the certificate came back it showed his birth mother's name not as Mavis Bovis as he had always thought, but Doris.

Michael had not seen his natural brother for many years, and asked me to ask his birth mother in spirit for some clue as to where Tony might be, which I did. In due course I received another message from Doris. It was simply a name: 'Stelforth'. This meant nothing to Michael, so I decided to try a search on the Internet, first with the name 'Bovis.' When I tapped it into 'Genes Reunited.' one lady kept popping up. I thought, what the heck, I'll email her, and ask if she knows Tony and Doris. Her reply came back: 'Yes, I do know a Tony he's my dad, but I don't know any Doris.' At the bottom she added, 'But I will contact my dad and ask if he knows her.'

I kept my fingers crossed - checking my emails every day, till two weeks later something came back, this time from the lady's father himself, 'Tony'. It was short and to the point:

'Dear Christina,

My daughter tells me you are looking for Tony Bovis – please tell me more.'

I emailed back, explaining about the birth certificate, and Michael, and the messages I had received from Doris, urging Michael to 'find Tony.' Was he that Tony, I asked - Doris's son, and thereby Michael's long lost brother? The reply came straight back: 'Guilty as charged,' he wrote, 'Yes, I'm Michael's brother.'

Spirit had put the two brothers in contact. All thanks to their mother Doris, who had had to give her boys up when they were young, and gone to spirit full of remorse for it. Michael and Tony later found out they had other brothers, and a sister too. They went on to make contact and have all since met up. Doris's fondest wish had been to see her children reunited, and now she had done it, her spirit could rest in peace.

In terms of my vocation, what though lay ahead for me now? I was appearing regularly on platform in front of the public, though never alone. I felt reassured to be always under the wing of another medium. Those who did work solo seemed to have some invisible source of confidence that was out of reach for me.

I was learning too that medium-ship could be a close-knit world, and among the many lovely people, I still saw myself both as a novice, and an outsider, not a real established medium with independent status. Perhaps this was to be my destiny, or perhaps some other role awaited me. If so, should I try to find it, or would it find me?

One night, while still in the spiritualist church circle, I had a strange dream. In this dream I was a man, riding a motorcycle at high speed along a country lane, accelerating ever faster as the bike hurtled round the narrow bends. Approaching a hill I suddenly lost control, came flying off the road and hit a tree. At the moment of impact I felt my spirit leave my body, which I saw, still that of the man, laying by the side of the road.

My spirit now rejoined my own body and, as myself Christina again, I climbed the hill. Down on the other side I saw crowds of people, all just standing there. From out of the crowd, two young girls came running up the hill towards me. When they reached me they grabbed hold of my hand. I recognised these children. They led me to a white building. Inside was a white table, and on it a white telephone. Everything in there was very bright. I could make out figures, queuing to make a telephone call.

Then someone came and greeted me, a black gentleman wearing a white suit. He said to me, 'Listen to the call.' I picked up the white telephone and heard children crying for their dad that had just gone to spirit, the man in the motorbike accident.

The black gentleman then said to me, 'You are that telephone call, you are the phone between this world and the next.' I did not say a word. 'Follow me,' he said, and led me to another place, a huge building with steps in front, like an Indian temple I climbed the steps and entered. In front of me were three men, like a judge and jury in a court of law. 'Sit,' said the man in the middle. 'Am I dead?' I asked. 'No,' he replied, 'you are neither dead nor alive. You are between the two worlds, you have work to do.' It was at this point I woke up.

The dream seemed to be asking, or more like telling me my role on earth, the scene in the temple not so much a selection panel as a trial. But how was I was supposed to plead, what action should I now take? My calling had been reaffirmed, but still I knew not where to go from here. I was approaching a crossroads. Only time and spirit would show me which direction to take.

Twenty-Five

It was June 2005, and I had been working as a medium alongside Michael for two years. The routine was for me to accompany him to whatever spiritualist or clairvoyant event he had been booked for, and go up on platform with him as and when appropriate. If Michael was the principal medium for the evening, the main attraction if you like, then I suppose I was like the support act.

Sometimes I was the 'roadie' too, and depending on our venue for the night, I would pick Michael up in my car at a convenient spot en route. One day, with Michael due to appear at an event in Broadstairs, I agreed to meet him at the railway station and go on to the centre from there. On the night, allowing plenty of time, I parked up and waited for his train to arrive. It pulled in right on schedule, but when the passengers had all got off there was no sign of Michael. He knew my car, and being a light summer evening there was no chance he couldn't see me, or me him.

I phoned his mobile number but there was no reply, so presumably his battery was low or he couldn't get a signal. There was still plenty of time to get to the venue, and thinking he must have simply missed his train, I sat tight and waited for the next one. It came in and once more I scanned the alighting passengers. Still there was no sign of Michael. Worried now, I tried his mobile again, and sent repeated texts, but there was no response.

It was now coming up to 6.45, and we were due on platform at 7.30. It would take time to get to the venue and get settled in. Even if we set off now we'd be cutting it fine. I thought, oh my god, all those people are going to be sitting there waiting, some perhaps anxious and hoping to hear from spirits tonight, they're going to be let down. I had to make a decision. Did I sit tight and wait still longer for Michael, 'phone someone at the venue to explain and then go home, or go along in person and say sorry, there would be no clairvoyance tonight. Either way there were going to be a lot of disappointed people. Though there was one other option. I started my engine and turned out of the car park.

I arrived at the venue at 7.25. The room was virtually full, and with five minutes to go, the organisers were looking anxiously at their watches.

'Where's Michael?' asked the president.

'I'm sorry, I don't know.' I replied breathlessly, 'something must have happened.'

'Will you be all right, to go on without him?'

'Yes. I'll be all right.'

The words were confident, I wasn't. As I made my way to the front the conversations tailed off, the shuffling and fidgeting quietened, and all eyes were on me. The 'show' was about to begin. Stepping onto the platform, I made a silent prayer asking spirit to guide and help me through what I was about to do, conduct an evening of clairvoyance, in public, for the first time, entirely on my own.

I needn't have worried. Contacts came to me rapidly and in abundance, and the audience that night were not disappointed, particularly those for whom there were words of comfort or reassurance, or whose loved ones on the other side simply made their presence known through me. Spirit had not let me down, and deeming I was ready to move on, had once again arranged for it to happen.

One morning, later that same year, I had a phone call from another medium. She and her partner had been due to appear together at an afternoon of clairvoyance at the Star of the East in Broadstairs. Unfortunately, she said, her partner couldn't make it now, and would I step in? It was short notice, and again I felt very unsure, but somehow I couldn't say no.

As I stood on platform, I saw a petite lady in spirit, standing next to an elderly gentleman in the congregation. I turned towards him and said, 'I'm coming to you sir,'

'Thank you,' he replied, looking at me expectantly.

'I have someone here for you - a lady, your wife.'

'Oh – oh yes, thank you...' Spirit began speaking – something about "night".

Then I heard her more clearly; the word was "nightingales". 'She wants to give you "nightingales,"' I told the gentleman, not knowing what this meant.

He did. His eyes brimming, he said in an emotional voice, 'Oh! - That was our song – "A Nightingale Sang in Berkeley Square" – we always used to slow dance to it…'

More messages were coming through from the lady 'She's talking about her heart,' I said, 'and wants to say something to you – "I'm sorry I didn't tell you I was ill."' I said, 'She wants to tell you how much she loves you.'

The gentleman, the tears now rolling down his cheeks, nodded. Then the lady in spirit called out, 'Margaret, I'm Margaret.'

Crying, he replied, 'Margaret yes, that's my wife - Margaret….'

I was now seeing images of men in Royal Air Force uniforms, and heard names – first John –

'Yes, that's my brother.'

Then came David – 'Yes, David…' Then a lady named Joanie… 'Joanie's my sister…' He knew all of them.

At the end of the session the gentleman, whose name was Ernie, came up to me. 'I have been waiting for four years for my Margaret - you spoke just like her.'

Ernie would tell everyone about his reading, and how his beloved Margaret came through to him that afternoon in Broadstairs.

But there was more to come. One night, unable to sleep, I woke in a dream-like state to see another young man in Air Force uniform. This one I took to be the rank of corporal. Holding his hat politely in his hand, he gave me the message: 'Tell Ernie hello,' and his name, 'Coleman', then faded away.

I looked at my bedside clock. I had Ernie's telephone number, but it was still the middle of the night. I decided to call him in the morning, when hopefully the message would be welcomed. I was curious as to what the connection was, and why this particular spirit – a young man who, from his uniform, appeared to have passed over a long time ago

- should want Ernie to remember him. The next few hours were a blur, as I tried to keep the details of what I had seen clear in my mind, while drifting in and out of sleep.

At 8a.m. I dialled Ernie's number. 'Ernie,' I said, 'its Christina - I've had a visitor, someone with a message for you. An RAF corporal, he said, "Tell Ernie hello", and gave his name as Coleman.'

'Coleman?' repeated Ernie.

'Yes,' I said, 'Corporal Coleman.'

Ernie then shouted, 'Coleman – Corporal Coleman? Oh my god…oh my god!' He seemed both shocked and amazed.

'Ernie, are you OK?' I asked.

'Yes, yes,' he replied, 'Coleman…well I never.'

'And Ernie, he had taken off his hat, he was holding it - does that mean anything?'

On hearing this last piece of information, Ernie told me who the Corporal was, and how their destinies had been intertwined. It had happened during the Second World War, when Ernie and Corporal Coleman had been comrades serving their country together. Whilst overseas the pair had been part of a unit engaged in covert operations. One night, set to deploy, Corporal Coleman had woken Ernie in time to leave their position safely under cover of darkness, thereafter to embark on a boat and carry out their mission.

Following the successful deployment, Ernie had returned with his unit to base. Not everyone made it back to the boat however, and Ernie's friend Coleman was among those missing. Later the Corporal was discovered lying on the battlefield, minus his head, which had been blown clean off his body during the fighting.

As soldiers in small units often do, Ernie and Coleman had looked out for each other. Now Coleman was dead. For years Ernie had suffered the pangs of survivor guilt, the feeling he was unfairly privileged to have survived, while others, his friend Coleman included, died so horribly, and so very young.

Now decades later, the Corporal had come through to say hello to his comrade who had lived on. If he bore any grudge, he wouldn't have communicated in such positive way, and he had wanted Ernie to know that. There were no hard feelings, far from it. And by removing his hat, showing his head bare and very much intact, perhaps he was saying, this is how you remember me - and look, I'm fine.

Old soldiers never die they say, and this young one too, was very much still around to raise his hat to Ernie, as well as a smile. And, for Ernie and Margaret, the music still played. It was time once again, to take your partners ladies and gentlemen, for the slow dance…

"That certain night, the night we met,

There was magic abroad in the air,

There were Angels dining at the Ritz,

And a Nightingale sang in Berkeley Square."

Twenty-Six

It was two years before the next big shift in my life occurred, and this one was to be seismic. As with so many things, it seemed to come quite out of the blue, but the extent to which it changed my feelings about myself, as well as the scope, and direction of my work was to be truly extraordinary.

I often used to recall the day I came home and found my Mum reading the tealeaves, and of course, I had always known that a similar affinity with spirit was in me. As such things tend to run in families, it came as little surprise when my son Neil began to get interested in the paranormal. It was an interest we could obviously share, and we started going along together to various societies that studied and explored psychic happenings.

As Neil's fascination grew, he soon got the itch to start his own group, and together with his best friend Chris, invited people to join their newly formed KPH – the Kent Paranormal Hunters. The group's intentions were to find locations – old houses and other sites – that might possibly have some dramatic history attached to them – then to go along and see what voices, visions, or other spirit manifestations could be picked up on. After a look around on the net, Neil lighted on a place called Bretons Manor, a large old house in Essex that dated back to around 1740.

We booked a visit to the Manor for nine KPH members, to stay there overnight from the 7th to the 8th September. We arrived at about 10.30 on the Friday evening as arranged and were met in the car park by a guy called Bill who was head of the Essex and Kent Paranormal Research Society. Bill was a striking figure, with combed back grey hair, and dressed all in black. 'Derek Acorah look-alike,' I whispered to Neil as we went in.

Bill took us over to the old barn, where we were split into groups and, over a cup of tea, told what was expected of us. I was placed in Bill's group. Soon it was time to go over to the Manor and begin. Making our way through the rambling old house, lots of contacts came through to me. To save the experience for those who have yet to visit Breton,

I won't say what spirits and secrets were uncovered that night, but there were plenty. When we were finally done in the small hours, Bill congratulated us on our findings.

Bill, though not a psychic himself, had worked in the paranormal field for many years, since having a personal experience with spirit at the age of seventeen. It was through Bill, that I was one day asked to attend and read at his local spiritualist church. This was destined to take my work into a whole new dimension. In fact it would completely transform me. For the first time in my life I was about to know what it meant to be special, to be valued.

Before going on platform I was as always quite nervous. Bill, seeking to give me confidence, had a word in my ear. 'People love you!' he said.

'Love me?' I replied, 'No one's ever really loved me.'

Bill said, 'Believe it – you are loved.'

With that I walked to the platform, and as I stood up I had this incredible feeling, which I can only describe as overwhelming love. At the same time I felt every kind of related emotion – pain, sorrow, pity, joy, remorse, pathos, ecstasy, all of these things and more, transcending into this pure, beautiful, all-embracing love. I wanted to hold each and every person there in that room, gather them in my arms and take care of them. I really, really loved them, and this love was coming from spirit, these peoples' loved ones were showing me what it was to be truly loved.

To this day I have problems believing what happened that evening. I had been given signs before, guiding me towards my vocation, reminders to keep on with the journey, to develop what abilities I had, not, as in the parable of the talents, to bury them.

But this had been more than a sign. The Bible refers to epiphany, the unmistakable manifestation of Christ or spirit in the world. With no wish to be irreverent, the absolute love that came to me that evening felt like a religious experience, a moment of epiphany.

I was to see even more how Bill had played a part in this change. Later on he wrote this report of the first time I met him, our visit to Bretons Manor.

'The first team to come to Bretons was Kent Paranormal, run by Christina's son Neil Green. ...When KPH arrived we invited them into the barn for tea and a chat till the Manor was empty. When the investigation was about to start, KPH split into three small teams, accompanied by two of our team (just as guides).

This turned out to be great, as she is an excellent medium, the best I've ever seen. Since the first time we investigated Bretons, we have had a number of mediums on our investigations, most of which were good, and picked up on some of the same things that are at the manor. Christina picked up on all of them and much more – all were validated in the history of the property that couldn't be found on the net.

I myself have been to many meetings at spiritualist churches, and I can tell someone who's a fake, and who's not. I saw promise, and knew this lady has a real gift, so I told my spiritualist church about her.'

What a favour that referral turned out to be; though favour is completely the wrong word; it was so much more. My work took a quantum leap. Bill opened further doors for me, he made introductions and created opportunities to work ever more closely with spirit. He gave me encouragement, and belief in myself.

There is something special between us. He is my rock, but there's much more to our relationship; the romance, the laughter we share, and the kind of energy, rapport, complete understanding, affection and trust that can't be explained, you just know. It was a bonding of spirits, the recognition of a common purpose. The love is strong between us. Bill is the catalyst, and he continues to be the generous soul and the inspiration in my life. We look to the future together; a soul partner, he showed me what love is. Thank you Bill.

REGRETS

'I'm sorry' 'I didn't say goodbye' 'I never told you I loved you'. Such thoughts often haunt us when loved ones have died. The pain of grief is laced with that terrible thing called regret, and it can cut like a knife. To know we can never say the kind and loving things we ought to have said, perform those small thoughtful acts we now so wished we had, for the person we held so dear.

Worse still may be the memory of hurtful words we uttered to our loved ones in moments of anger, tiredness or folly, and which we never found the time or chance to take back. How those words turn to ashes in our mouths now. Perhaps we were too proud to say sorry. If so, how ashamed and wretched we feel for having been so small minded, so petty. And to someone we loved. Death puts all of us in our place.

'If only' we say to ourselves over and over again 'Too late' echoes in our heads. These must be two of the saddest phrases in the English language.

How many of us have caused unhappiness to another by our actions? Maybe it was a friend we upset, or a passer-by, unkind words brought on by frustration or selfishness, or because we were in a hurry or upset about something ourselves.

Harsh words can be infinitely more painful when directed at those closest to us. 'You always hurt the one you love' they say, and how true that can be. When the loved one is suddenly no longer around, the significance of what we have done hits home with a vengeance. Our sense of regret wakes us up with a shock, forcing us to confront ourselves, and the consequences of our behaviour on others.

The same can apply the other way round. The departed might have caused distress to us or other members of their family, and gone to their grave with the matter still outstanding. The slight may have been nothing specific; relationships cool over time, people grow apart and 'not speaking' sets in. In many a falling out, no one could ever quite recall what it was all about. But a storm in a teacup can still cause a shipwreck in a family. The habit of estrangement, once the loved one has died, can be as distressing as any actual quarrel we may have had with them.

When people come to someone like myself, a medium, they are often seeking to resolve these issues with their loved ones now in spirit. By making contact, they hope to put things right, to forgive, and, or be forgiven. Happily this can and does happen. And as much as those on earth earnestly desire to contact spirit and have closure on unfinished business, so spirit can seek to come though to the living and say their piece. Here too there can be fulfilment for both spirit and the living.

There can be complications however, usually arising when the two sides don't meet in the middle. Someone contacting from the earthly plane may not always be welcomed by the particular spirit they are seeking, and vice versa. Sometimes a spirit other than the one hoped for enters in, and asks the medium to communicate with the person having the reading. Sadly on occasions, that person has refused, and I have had to say no to spirit, I cannot pass on their message. Though spirit will stand back, or even leave if asked to, on days like this I am not immune to a sense of frustration, the feeling that I have failed. However I have to respect the wishes of both sides. In my role as a medium, the bringing together of the living and the dead is often the easy part. Reaching closure on some of the problems that divide them can be much harder.

One lady in particular comes to mind. So far hers has been the shortest reading I have ever given, but at the same time rather strange, and unpleasant. Another lady, whom I had read for on several occasions, had recommended me, and it was she who made the booking on her friend's behalf, We had therefore not met before the actual day of her reading, when at the appointed time my son Neil, who often acts as my host, showed her into my little church as I like to call it, on the side of the house.

Spirit began telling me that this lady had caused a lot of problems within her family. I was given some names, which when I passed them on seemed to make her uncomfortable. Then spirit told me there were difficult issues over a grandchild. Hearing this the lady grew more anxious still. 'Don't go there,' was all she would say.

There followed further revelations, which for confidentiality I will leave out. The important point was that contrary to what this lady might have thought, spirit had no grievances towards her, no axe to

111

grind. All they wanted to do was let her know they were watching over things, and hoping these protracted family problems would be resolved.

About ten minutes into the reading however, she suddenly stood up and said 'I'm not gong to listen to this!' and without another word stormed out of the door. Neil, my son, seeing her rush off down the path in such a state, came hurrying in to see if I was OK.

Later I phoned the lady's friend, the one who had referred her to me, and explained what had happened. Her friend tried to apologise, saying I was spot on about her not wanting to confront the situation. I told the friend not to worry, and said I was sorry for both spirit and the family, that an ideal opportunity to help both sides had not been taken.

As mediums we play the role of bringing people together, who otherwise would not be able to communicate, and hopefully allow them to lay to rest feelings of regret, resentment or hatred. Spirit will always be there, and will usually attempt to do what is right. Those on the earthly plane can be far more difficult to deal with. Understandably, they may be fearful of confronting painful issues, and in some cases refuse to come to terms with past or present conflicts and emotions.

One area where feelings of regret are particularly acute, often to the point of torment, is suicide. In my early days of medium-ship, I found this issue the most difficult of all to deal with when linking to spirit. Perhaps this was partly to do with what happened to my Linda. Although I have now learned to some extent to cope with the tidal wave of emotion that can threaten to overwhelm me during such readings, at one time I found the experience completely draining.

Once my own soul was, if you like open, all the feelings of the person who had committed suicide, and their loved ones here on earth, would rush in, like a dam breaking. Many times, before the relative or friend of the departed had even arrived to see me, I would already be getting this surge of emotion. Through spirit alone I would know the factual details of how they took their life, as well as feeling a proportion of the pain they had felt as their life ebbed away. A terrible sense of desolation would come over me. This I knew to be the feelings of the departed as the misery engulfed them, and, inwardly screaming for the pain to end, they contemplated the final leap into darkness.

Some say you can never tell who is most at risk of suicide. The truth must surely be that anyone is potentially vulnerable. Given the circumstances, anyone can sink low enough, to the point they simply don't want to go on. True, it's easy to miss or ignore the signals, to see other people's desperation as complaining, whining, moping. I wonder how many of us out there have commented to someone, even close family, 'Oh don't worry, you'll be fine.' Or, more dreadful still. 'What are you complaining about? There's a lot of people worse off!' Well, I have to admit I've made these kinds of remarks in the past, and had them made to me. But believe me, you couldn't say anything more pointless or hurtful.

For so many who are in desperate emotional plight, all the help in the world may not prevent a terrible outcome. It's as if their pain is beyond reach. But we must never give up if we feel someone might need us. Tell that person you are there for them, and tell them you love them. If it is too late to speak these assurances in the earthly plane, and, suffering grief and regret you come to a reading, be there for them now. Now is important too, for the departed soul may yearn to say sorry for what they did, to make some atonement for the hurt and misunderstanding they left behind, and perhaps to hear your penitence.

If not, those that have passed over by their own hand, and others who have left pain behind them, may carry their anguish forever. If those of us who remain don't help when a link is offered, these spirits only hope of relief, of moving on, may be when they return in another life. Death releases a person from earthly suffering, but if they have hurt us by going then we should forgive them, and let them know so.

And if the fault lies in ourselves still on earth, how do we stop regretting? That's like saying how do we stop being human. We always regret something, jus as we always desire something, and our emotions are forever trying to pull us this way and that. If we aim for perfection we will always fall short, but we can always strive to improve ourselves through our habits; of showing respect for others, of showing love. By remembering there won't always be a tomorrow, and for some that will come about much sooner.

So refrain from hurting your loved ones. And remember that hurtfulness can be indirect too, forgetting to say and do the little things that we ought. Give people a minute when they need it, we can all spare that however busy we are. Give your children a hug before they leave for school. Phone your mum or dad, your brother, your sister or the friend you fell out with. Don't say 'I'll do it tomorrow,' for who can be certain what tomorrow may bring. Don't let it be regret.

The Café

There was a lovely little café Mal and I used to go to back in 2005. We would usually drop in there after a visit to the gym. There's nothing like exercise for giving you an appetite, and having convinced ourselves we'd burned off a few calories, we would then feel OK about putting them back on again, and depending on the menu, a few more for good luck!

Apart from serving delicious food, the café had, for me, another quality about it. I don't know whether this was because it was close to particular leylines, which some people say have an effect on spirit, or if there was anything else unusual about the location, but for some reason I received all manner of contacts there. Let me take you there....

Scene One.

It's an ordinary morning in the café. A couple come in, well tanned and very relaxed. It doesn't need spirit to tell me they are just back from somewhere hot. In my head though, I am hearing more. I turn to Mal.

'They've been on holiday to Rhodes. They stayed at the Athena Hotel.'

Mal, being nosier than I am, gets into conversation with the couple. 'You look like you've been somewhere warm,' he says.

'Yes, Rhodes,' says the gentleman. We tell him we once considered Rhodes, but plumped for Corfu in the end.

'You should try Rhodes,' he replies 'apart from Falaraki, its quieter than Corfu.'

His other half agrees. 'Yes,' she says, 'we stayed at the Athena Hotel.'

Scene Two.

It is raining this morning, the café is quiet, hardly any customers. We order some food, and after chatting with the owner, whom we know, sit down near the bar area. Within a few minutes I begin to feel a touch nauseous, and put a hand to my stomach. An elderly couple have just come in and sat down opposite us.

The unpleasant sensation in my stomach is growing stronger now. My appetite has vanished, and I really want to leave. Leaning over I say quietly to Mal, 'See that poor lady? She has cancer of the liver, she's not long for this world.'

The discomfort in my stomach eases a little, but now I feel an overwhelming desire to go to the lady and put my arms round her, to hold and reassure her, take any fear of what is to come away from her.

It's at times like this that I am glad of Mal's common sense, knowing he will usually caution restraint, and not let me intrude. Not everyone in such circumstances would understand or accept why a complete stranger might want to hug them, and my advances might be very unwelcome. Apart from the possibility of adding to someone's distress, there's also the chance I might end up in trouble myself, men in white coats carting me off to padded rooms etc.

But returning to our elderly couple, the next thing that happens is the lady's husband goes up to the bar to order. 'A coffee for me please,' he says, 'and a soft drink for my wife.' He then adds, 'We've just had chemotherapy for liver cancer.' When he says 'we' I know what he means. 'She has to take her pills.'

I can sense her pain and sorrow, the sorrow of both of them, knowing she will soon have to leave him. My sorrow is that I cannot help. If only I could reassure them they will be together again, that this is not the end, merely a stopover on a long journey to heaven.

Scene Three.

I am eating more than I should today, but the food in this café is just so good! We are about to witness what many people experience, though most times are not fully aware of.

I am sitting with my back towards an elderly lady in a wheelchair. A younger lady with her addresses her as 'Mum' and there is a granddaughter with them too. I whisper to Mal. 'That lady in the wheelchair, her husband's here.'

A few seconds later, the lady's daughter sits bolt upright and gives a sort of shudder. 'Ooh!' she says, 'I felt as if someone just went right through me…'

Mal looks at me. 'I see you're tuned in on high frequency again today,' he murmurs.

It seems a shame the family are unaware Granddad is there, keeping his tender eye on them. But how wonderful for him, that he can see them! And who knows, perhaps deep down they do feel his presence. It is often the way when families are close, when there is love.

Well, that was then. Mal and I don't go to the café any more. I imagine the spirits are still looking in though.

Are You a Sceptic?

It's OK to be a sceptic, not so good to be a cynic. Cynics tend to discredit people and ideas whatever the evidence to the contrary. They make their minds up in advance, and don't really like to consider the possibility they could ever be wrong about anything. It can be hard work, being around this negative, clever-clever, attitude to life.

Sceptics on the other hand are more discerning. They're nobody's fools, and they can be mistaken for cynics. But the crucial difference is perhaps this; where a cynic stubbornly turns his nose up at new ideas, a sceptic will say: 'It sounds far-fetched, but I suppose there could be something in it – I'd like to know more.'

The dictionary definition of a sceptic is: 'A person who generally doubts the accepted view.' Herein lies a problem for all mediums. Is the belief that certain people can communicate with the spirit world a generally accepted view? In our present day society, if you conducted a poll, it probably isn't.

From my own experience I would say people fall into one of three groups: 'Yes', 'Not sure', and 'Not on your life.'

The 'Yes' group have no doubts. They tend to be from the older generation, and have had psychic experiences of their own or readings from mediums. They fully accept the existence of a spirit world, and believe that a good medium has the ability to contact that world.

Our next group, the 'Not sure', are like so many people on polling day – uncertain which way to cast their vote - or whether to abstain.

Finally we come to the 'No on your life' group, who, when asked if they would ever go to a medium, reply – you've guessed it…

As mediums we should not set out to convert anyone. Trying to convince cynics and sceptics alike with scientific 'proof', is probably impossible, and not the role of a good medium. Our work is what it is. It is for those we read for, and rests on the quality of what they experience.

Those who start out 'Not sure' can of course become believers. But equally if things go wrong for them they may join the 'Not on your life' brigade. Which way they eventually swing, can depend entirely on their experience with the medium that conducts their first reading. If on that visit nothing comes through that they can relate to, and the reading is in truth no better than guesswork, then it's very likely they'll go away feeling not only disappointed, but inclined to think the whole notion of a spirit world ridiculous.

And of course they will tell their friends as much. This can have far-reaching consequences, as it discredits medium-ship in general. For some reason, one poor experience with a medium has a tendency to cast the whole practice in a negative light, and puts people off who might otherwise benefit from a reading.

The lucky person who finds a good medium, and has that contact with a loved one they so longed for, will go away maybe tearful, but also uplifted. The 'Not sure' person now becomes a member of group one, the 'Yes' people, not because he or she is gullible, but because they have experienced the presence of spirit for themselves.

In conducting a good reading, the medium likewise gains fulfilment, and if the person they've read for tells their friends, the positive reports are likely to bring more people along. As in any walk of life, word of mouth recommendation for a medium is worth its weight in gold.

Now we come to the last group, the 'Not on your life' lot. These in turn fall into two types. There are those who simply have no interest in the spirit world, and of course that's entirely their right. Like I say, no one should be out to preach, and with people that would never go near a medium, there isn't an issue to deal with. It's simply a case of live and let live.

Then there are those who actively seek to discredit mediums, who set out to prove that we are either deluded or a bunch of charlatans and fakes, exploiting the vulnerability of others for our own gain. They may pride themselves that no one can 'put one over' on them, and many would remain stubborn non-believers even if spirit were to bite their proverbial behinds.

Quite often, a sceptic, or even the most stubborn cynic will, against their better judgment, find themselves unwillingly face to face with a medium. An interested relative suggests they attend a platform event or have a personal reading, or maybe a friend drags them along to a Spiritualist church one evening. If they do turn up, it is either to see the medium fail, or to satisfy the wife, husband, girlfriend or whoever, and get home as quickly as possible with the minimum embarrassment.

As much as these people can be hard work, and often quite rude, I accept them as a challenge, and I know it's the same for the spirits out there who may wish to contact them. In the living world, do we not all long to be noticed, to be thought about, to feel we matter to somebody? Why should the spirit world be any different? Spirits want to come through, and they want loved ones to know they are there. Being a cynic or a sceptic won't stop them. In fact spirit often seems to relish the task of showing us what they can do, proving to us they are there, and that they know things.

I would like now to share a couple of stories with you, true tales of my encounters with sceptics.

The first concerns a gentleman who came for a reading at the request of his wife. The couple attended together at a platform event, and as the reading proceeded he was very non-committal, his only response to what I was telling him being an occasional shrug of the shoulders. I had given him several pieces of information about his deceased brother, including his name, and how and where he died. I also told him the nickname he had for his brother - 'Grumpy.'

After a few minutes he said, 'If you're that good, what colour shoes was my brother wearing when he was buried?'

'Brown,' I replied. 'And actually they were not on him at his burial. You're wearing them.'

Not denying this, he looked down for a moment, then said, 'OK, what have I got in my wallet? - Oh, and anyone could say "money."'

'You have a small piece of paper,' I replied, 'that you have folded over at the corners until it's really small. It was to write a phone number on.'

'All right then, what's the number?'

'There is no number,' I said, 'your brother died before he gave it to you, which is why you kept the paper.'

At this point his wife said, 'Let's have a look then.'

Reluctantly he took out his wallet. Tucked down inside it, no bigger than a postage stamp, was a scrap of paper, which when unfolded, was shown to be blank on both sides. Without saying another word, the gentleman then put the scrap of paper back in his wallet and walked out of the hall.

At the end of the evening he returned. Coming up to me he said, 'Sorry, I would never have believed someone could do that. Thank you.'

Being probably his first experience with a medium, and not being his idea to attend, it was natural for this gentleman to be defensive during the reading. And then to hear a stranger reveal accurate details about his dead brother, someone whom he obviously held very dear, must have felt intrusive to say the least. He didn't have to come back and say what he did to me. I admired his honesty and courage in doing so.

Although many of the stories I could tell you concern people's grief, there are some I can't help but smile about. One was close to home, about Mal in fact, and goes back to the time we were married. Mal has had his sceptical tendencies regarding the spirit world in the past, but has gradually changed his mind. So what convinced him? The following episode probably gave a helping hand, or should I say handshake.

One morning I told him he was going to have his hand shaken that day.

'Really?' he replied, implying there was nothing very surprising about this prediction

'You're also going to receive some money,' I said, '£200.' He looked more interested now, then laughed and said, 'Sack and pay-off more like!'

That evening Mal came home from work smiling. He told me his manager had asked to see him. Congratulating him on ten years service with the firm, he had warmly shaken his hand. 'So I thought you might want to treat yourself,' he said, presenting me with some shopping vouchers.

'You must be in the money!' I said.

'Yes,' he said, 'the boss gave me a little cheque – two hundred quid!'

For another tale, let's go to my local gym, you remember, the one Mal and I used to frequent a few times a week, so we could eat more at the café. Anyway, there was this chap we used to see at the gym, a retired gentleman, but one clearly determined age should be no barrier to an incredible body, in fact seeing him train you'd think he wanted to be the next Incredible Hulk.

But he always had time for a chat, to tell the truth once you set him off he could talk for Britain. When conversing he would come up really close, the odour of sweat and sour breath competing with his biceps to see which was stronger.

What fascinated me about him though, was that I was getting a psychic connection to someone called Dorothy, and the image of a blue summer dress. I told Mal, who as usual wanted to jump straight in, and ask him outright who Dorothy was. I said to hold back, and that I thought there was a conflict involved here, a sense of something not quite right. But no matter how much I asked spirit, I couldn't get a clear picture of this Dorothy, or the dress, or what the connection was.

Every time we visited the gym and saw this gentleman, we became more curious about his mysterious Dorothy. The weeks went by, and still I was seeing only hazy images of him and her, and the blue dress.

'Just ask him, I'm sure he won't mind,' Mal kept saying.

'No, no,' I would always reply, 'let's just leave it, maybe it'll work itself out in time.'

It did. In fact one day I had the most crystal clear picture come through. 'I'm glad we didn't say anything to him,' I said to Mal when I knew. 'What do you mean?' he replied. I told him what I had seen.

'So you're saying…ah-hah yes I see, well that would fit in.' he said.

'Let's not mention it though when we see him.'

'But then how will you know if you're right?'

A few months later I was in my local charity shop browsing the ladies wear when someone bumped into me. Looking round I saw a figure in a lovely blue summer dress and hat.

'Oops, so sorry,' came the apology.

'That's all right,' I said then looked again. It was our friend from the gym. He had recognised me now.

Without missing a beat he said, 'Oh hello! How are? How's your training going? I should be down there myself today really, only honestly I've had so much to do this morning, what with this that and the other…'

I had met Dorothy at last.

Life

We have spoken much about the after-life - now let us consider life itself.

These words came to me:

The most beautiful gift is a new life, to hold the newborn in your arms.

God must have felt the same. Imagine the creation of life itself.

Imagine how proud Our Lord must have felt having created our world.

His child was without sin. We know we came from another world, the spirit world.

How often do we hear the parent say of the child: 'He's very knowing.'

Or, 'He's an old soul.' That beautiful baby - without sin or worries

But what else was he told to expect?

Imagine how many are taking care of each of us in the spirit world.

We have our loved ones there, loved ones who also have experienced this world. They watch over us, but they cannot intervene. They can guide us, but they cannot change what's to be.

Life. It's not only the newborn children, look at what's around us, the beauty of our world, the green grass, the trees and flowers. Yes, how proud Our Lord must have felt. So why do we destroy it – greed, depravity? It breaks my heart to see conflict – from couples arguing to countries fighting, tanks and guns and bombs doing unspeakable things to people. All the while, the innocent baby is born, to a world no longer so. The Lord must look upon us and say 'Why? My creation is destroying its home, the perfect earth I toiled for my children to live in is no more.'

People often say: 'If there is a God, why doesn't he stop these horrors?'

But God did not bring about these things, we did. It is for us to put an end to them.

Linda

When my sister Linda passed away on April 16th 2003, it left a hole in my heart and my life that will never be filled. In our years growing up together, we had our ups and downs, our differences, large and small, but we were always close, as sisters should be.

Getting into our early teens, with different jobs, then husbands, our paths diverged. My job took me for long periods all over the country, while Linda remained in our old stamping ground. Lazy as it sounds, if we'd had email and the social networking sites of today, we may have kept in touch more often. Not that it mattered in the end for Linda and I. However long the period of separation, however far the physical distance between us our friendship remained intact, and our bond unbreakable.

Death is the ultimate separation, the remotest distance. Having got my sister back, she was all too soon taken from me again, not for a holiday, or a job, or moving house, but forever. There would be no more chats, shared tears or laughter. No more my pal to go shopping with, or just being there for each other.

Before Linda died, on the dark days when she said she couldn't go on, she also promised me she would never really be gone, but always close by. One little sign or message, she said, and I would know she was there.

It might seem a wonderful thing to be able to communicate directly with our loved ones who have died. But as a medium I have strong reservations about this. If we were able to talk with them, if it were anything like my Linda and I, we would want to be chatting all the time. I would want answers from her – why did she leave me, what was it like where she was, and why couldn't she come back? Most worrying of all, in moments of despair I might feel an irresistible urge to pass over myself and be with her, without any thought of the consequences.

But to this day nothing has come through. As I progress on this journey, I increasingly believe that no sign will come from Linda. In my heart, I think I know that we can never have direct contact from the spirit world with our immediate family.

In my own case, it has not happened through any other medium either, and I have been to a few.

Even though I know that the life beyond is real, I believe we must accept the separation of our physical, earthly existence, from the world of spirit. We must wait our turn, and finish our tasks here before we enter that realm.

I do feel that the spirit world protects us by only allowing contact through a neutral third party – a medium. This way, the sanity of the living is maintained. The alternative, whereby we could call up our relatives on the other side at will, would, surely be unthinkable, the whole world walking around like those people who talk into their mobile phones all day.

How many questions do we ask ourselves in the course of a day? Without realising it we are asking questions all the time.

What shall I eat tonight? Will it rain? Should I take the car, or will I want a drink? Does he like me? Do his parents like me? Should I change my job? Is my mum in heaven? Does she know I loved her really? Is my dad going to die soon? Is there really a God? Should I wear trousers or a skirt? Does my bum look big in this…?

Like a tape constantly rewinding in our heads, the questions go round and round, big and small, trivial and fundamental, the personal and the universal. When you think about it, our entire lives are made up of questions – a search for understanding, knowledge, answers, some of which are within our grasp, while others seem always out of reach.

The question on so many people's minds when they first consider going to a medium is, 'Can anyone really speak with the dead.' As you will already have gathered, I prefer the word 'spirit', but while people are still uncertain, they like to call a spade a spade. For me no such doubt exists. The spirit world is as real in its way as the world we inhabit, and yes, we can have communication with those who have passed over.

I could recount so many more stories, enough to fill several books, to show that for me, and many others the spirit world is not only real, but also very active.

One Thursday evening in May 2007, I was expecting two ladies for readings, one at 7.30, one at 8.30. Earlier in the day however, events had been set in motion that I had no knowledge or control over, but most certainly spirit knew what to do.

Each morning I like to get out my diary then check my emails and phone messages, to make sure I've not missed any appointments or enquiries. I know the spirit world doesn't sleep, and judging by the times of day and night people contact me about readings, it seems a lot of the living don't either - not that I'm complaining!

Anyway, opening my diary I saw that Carol and Jane were due at 7.30 and 8.30 respectively that evening. As I held the page open, the phone on my desk rang. It was Carol. After chatting for a couple of minutes, she said, 'Is there any chance you could fit me in for a reading?'

Assuming she meant rearrange the time, I said, 'Yes of course - that was good timing, I was just looking at your appointment in the diary.'

Carol however sounded baffled. 'You can't have been,' she said, 'I haven't made an appointment. I've only just got your number.'

Now I was baffled. 'Well I've got you down here – Carol - and your number,' I said, and read out the telephone number I had written beside her name in my diary.

'Yes that's my number,' she said, 'but I never gave it to you. I've never even spoken to you before. I only decided to call you a few moments ago. Someone who had seen you recommended you. I don't know her very well – Jane I think her name is – oh hang on, maybe she told you about me, is that what's happened?'

'No,' I said. 'Jane booked a reading for herself about two weeks ago. But she's never mentioned you.'

Carol couldn't understand why or how she could already be in my diary when I had never even heard of her till that moment. Not only her name but also her phone number, correct to the last digit. Still confused, she booked an appointment for a later date. During that reading, light was thrown on her considerable problems, and it was clear why she had been directed to a medium.

That direction had only one source. The other lady, Jane, had definitely made no mention of any Carol, nor had anyone else. I knew there was no way I could have written her name and exact telephone number down other than through the intervention of spirit. It was like a fail-safe; Carol had turned out to have serious needs, and if she had procrastinated about addressing them, i.e. not rung, I already had her number, and an appointment.

Christmas

How can you tell when it's Christmas? Because Woolworth's have got Easter eggs in the window! It's an old joke, and even staler now good old Woolies is no longer with us. But it highlights the way Christmas has become just another spending spree, which seems to start earlier each year.

The pressures this can put on families is well known. People usually want to give their children the best possible time at Christmas, but it isn't always so easy. Which probably accounts for the fond memories of 'the good old days', when an apple and a stick of chocolate in your stocking was enough to delight.

Christmas is a time for parties, for laughter, for sharing. But for so many it can be a time of misery, loneliness and despair. Some are having their first Christmas without their husband or wife, looking back at old photos for comfort, or a child's gifts remain unopened because tragedy has struck. Reliving happier times in the memory brings a smile, till the bitter reality of loss returns.

Then there are the families who have split up acrimoniously, the children that do not see their mum or dad, brother or sister, the partners that quarrel, the parent who's in prison. Lack of money, lack of love, lack of ordinary human warmth and companionship; these things seem the cruellest of all at Christmas time.

At Christmas, remember those in loveless relationships, most of all the children. Remember the lonely, especially the elderly, and do what you can for them, they may not be here next year.

If you have lost loved ones, send them a message this Christmas, to let them know you care, and are thinking of them. The Church may be closed, but spirit always listens, especially at Christmas.

John McDonald

We all like to complain. But how many of us have sat down and really thought about all the things we moan about - traffic, weather, the government, our little aches and pains and ailments, our disappointments and frustrations. So many of our complaints are so trivial, really. We may occasionally show concern for a friend who is ill or in trouble, we may dip our hand in our pocket for family, friends or famine relief now and again, but if we're honest, it's our own woes that concern us most of the time.

It's to be expected, with all the readings I do for people, that I come across more grief and sadness than in most lines of work. One man who remains strong in my memory is John McDonald. His character, and his outlook on life, touched me deeply. In a brief phone conversation with John, we had arranged a time and place for me to read for him, and I was at that point unaware of the experience that awaited me.

John greeted me at his home, his cheery disposition belying the fact he was not a well man. But I felt very much at ease with his soul, and with the spirits I could already sense around me. Before we had even sat down, I had his parents coming through. I held this back, allowing time for John and I to first settle in his lounge.

Despite his uncomplaining manner, it was obvious as he tried to get comfortable that John was having difficulty breathing. Meanwhile I could feel his parents' spirits around us growing more insistent, clamouring to impart so many things to me all at once.

As we began, it was his parents who told me that John was currently recuperating from cancer. Previously he had lost a kidney, as well as suffering cirrhosis of the liver, sadly without the compensation that enjoyment of wine had caused the problem, since he drank nothing stronger than tea. That would be bad enough news or most of us, but now John's blood count was seriously off, and more tests and hospital trips were on the cards.

All this information came from spirit, from John's mother and father. When it was passed on to him, his tears and nods of assent confirmed everything. The tears though were not for his personal predicament, but for his dear mum and dad passed over, in particular his sorrow that he had not been there for either of them at the end.

John's parents told me to assure him they had no regrets, and they were proud of him, not simply as their son, but because of his endless thought for others before himself. He had spent so much time helping other people, often in far-flung places around the world, with no concern for his own comfort or needs, that it had eventually taken its toll on him. In his commitment to the service of others, he had sacrificed not only his own health, but, unintentionally, neglected his own family too.

This is where John's soul touched mine, for spirit knew what he had done for others. His family had a place reserved for John, somewhere far beyond, where one day, they would all be reunited. But for now that journey was on hold. John, despite occasionally feeling, and wishing it were time to move on, was not finished with this life yet.

I sat with John for an hour. Not once did he complain, or express any kind of lament for his own situation. What was plain was his overriding concern for other people, including his parents on the other side. Several times spirit told me for John, 'Not yet, not yet. There is more in your earth journey – more help for others, more time that your soul is required here.'

Through all the difficulties, all the bad times he'd endured, I felt the presence of John's soul, shining through, unwavering and steadfast in its certainty of eternal life. With his care for both the living and the departed, it was as if he were doing two jobs, living parallel lives, the earthly and the spiritual.

When I left and went back to my car, I sat and closed my eyes for a few moments in quiet prayer. I thanked spirit for their connection with John, and asked that his journey be fruitful and fulfilling.

Every day we have our grumbles, our little Victor Meldrew moments, but I hope we can also try to see life as John did. I don't hold with saying, 'There's always someone worse off.' It's a pointless comparison to people in real trouble. But it is true that some of those who are worse off don't see it that way. They live their lives for others, and that is their salvation. God bless you John, and may your soul venture on.

Love

Love is a simple word, but it can mean so many things. Do we really understand it? How many songs feature the word 'Love' in the title? Thousands probably. Most often it refers to the relationship between two people, an infatuation, a love affair or married love. Do we say 'I love you' too often, or not enough? I think, not often enough, where we ought to.

When I first married Mal, I revelled in the fact of being 'Mrs Green'. At the same time, I felt I didn't know how to love. I would fear my husband, and keep him at arms' length. Mal was the same. I felt he treated me like a child - a kiss on the forehead before leaving the house, him controlling the finances, and no joint bank account. But then I was very naïve. Being in the armed forces, Mal had not only seen the world, but also its darkest side, warfare.

Mal made me feel safe, comfortable. But then things took a turn for the worse, and it all went down hill. Mal was still working, but I became the main breadwinner. The opportunity of being in a film in America was one that Mal urged me to take, but in my opinion for the wrong reason, i.e. money alone.

Faced with the prospect of spending a year away from my young son just to bring in money I simply couldn't do it. Mal, being very much a 'man's man' and very practical, couldn't see the problem. Feeling he neither understood, nor loved me anymore, I upped sticks and took little Neil with me.

Mal has often said to me how he regrets that time, and I know he does. But Mal and I have always been there for each other. He has remained a close friend, and in his own way I know he loved me. I also know he wants me to work for spirit, because he has seen the good it can bring about. He has been a great encouragement in writing my book. For all your help and support, thank you Mal.

I mentioned earlier how I had never felt loved till I began working seriously as a medium. This is true in one sense, in that after my dad died when I was twelve years old, life became very hard without him, and the feeling of being lonely and unloved intensified.

But there is more than one kind of love. The love of a mother for her child is perhaps the purest form of human love. In this imperfect world I have seen parents hurting their children, children hurting their parents. But when it begins, that relationship is surely perfect.

I know I loved my dad, and my mum, and still do. I know they loved me, though with my mum it wasn't easy for her to show it when we were growing up. I will always love my sister Linda too of course, deeply. I have also talked of the love that surrounded me that night when I got up on platform to read. This was of a different quality, a kind of universal, transcendent love - the love of God perhaps, which is by definition perfect, flowing through everyone who was present in that room.

But the greatest feeling of love I have ever experienced, was when my son Neil was born. For the first time in my life I felt I had a reason to live. I wanted to protect him from the pain of this world. Looking down at him in my arms, I would also think: he won't love me when he is older, but I will love him, and show him I love him. The midwife used to get angry with me. 'Put your baby down,' she would say, 'you're making a rod for your own back as a mother.' This was the received wisdom at that time – let your baby cry, don't keep picking them up. But I would hold on to my baby for as long and as often as I could, and it has been the same with all my other children.

My fears were unfounded, for I know that my children do love me. Neil, now a grown man, is very protective of his mother. My younger ones still have some growing to do, but I hope they too have the feeling of being loved and wanted, and that this will stay with them. I love my children more than life itself. I'm lucky, because they have supported me on my journey. I thank God because if it wasn't for them, I know I wouldn't be here.

Why did it take me so long to believe I was worthy of love? I never take anything for granted, and I know it could all end tomorrow, but I will continue to work for spirit. All the while I have breath in my body.

Afterthoughts on the Afterlife

'Oh, she's a mind reader…' That's what many people believe mediums do, and there can be some confusion between what is telepathy and what is medium-ship. Strangely though, those who are sceptical of mediums will often quite readily accept the practice of mind reading. So these people believe that thoughts can be invisibly transferred, though only between those who are living. But if a thought is invisible, why should it be dependent on the physical life or death of the person thinking it?

These are probably questions for advanced philosophers, and it's all too easy to stray out of our depth when trying to analyse the subject. Attempting to rationalise the existence of the spirit world can send you round in circles, like a dog chasing its tail. The only real proof is in actual experience, what individual people hear and see through their medium.

There have always been sceptics and cynics, and there always will be. At one time mediums and others who worked with spirit were called witches and, through fear and ignorance, persecuted. Official witch-finders were sent out to hunt down anyone thought to 'have the devil' in them, torture them, and put them to death. Even the sin of keeping a cat could be enough for sentence to be pronounced on some harmless woman. Fortunately we live in more enlightened times. Though many still view mediums with suspicion, no one wants to burn us at the stake any more.

Atheists do not believe we exist after death. Yet why aren't they afraid of dying? Perhaps they are. My view is this: when we are in spirit, both before and after death, we know that our existence goes on, we see if you like, both sides of the curtain. While on earth, we are given the choice to believe in the spirit world or not. Given the complex and busy nature of our life on the earthly plane, it is not surprising that many have no concern with the afterlife. As we grow older though, our attitude often changes. With age comes increased curiosity about the big questions, the biggest of all being life and death, what happens to us after the grave. When we ourselves lose a loved one, it can be a watershed in our thinking. Suddenly we want to know: where is that person now?

It doesn't always happen that way of course, and some remain cynics to the last. But why, near the end of their life, do so many people cry out to their loved ones in spirit? It is because their belief has finally returned. 'The prospect of death wonderfully concentrates the mind.' So said Sir Thomas Moore sentenced to execution by Henry the Eighth for refusing to renounce his Catholic faith. Imminent death must also tend to free the spirit, allowing it to see the true reality, that of moving on to something beyond, the life hereafter.

Life itself is a mystery, why should death be any different? The greatest puzzle for many is why God would create something so beautiful as life, only to destroy it by making us die. The spirit world provides an explanation, the notion that after our physical death we pass to another kind of existence. This is the basis of Christian teaching.

'But I'm sorry, I still don't believe there's an afterlife. When you're dead you're dead, end of story.'

We often hear this, and fair enough, each to his or her opinion. But imagine how frustrating it must be for someone on the other side, yearning to give a message to their beloved son, daughter, grandson, niece, husband or wife, brother or sister. Or perhaps the unbeliever is the spirit's mother or father - a sad thing to outlive one's own children, but of course it happens, often in tragic circumstances. That dead child, or whoever, may be desperate to connect with their loved ones left behind.

So if you don't believe, please at least try, if only for the sake of others. And if you are already a believer, please don't discriminate. A lady phoned me and said, 'I'd like a reading but I only want one particular person to come through.'

This always upsets me because other spirits will so often appear. To turn them away seems rude apart from anything else. Next time you have a reading, and a friend or family member comes to you unexpectedly, don't shut the door in their face. Be as pleased as they are to say: 'I'm here for you,' because they are.

Let us pray for the living that don't believe, especially the bereaved as their grieving continues on earth, while spirit grieves, unable to give comfort.

And let us never forget to thank God for allowing those loved ones to come through, and giving to all his children the comfort they need.

Dear Heavenly Father,

Please bless each and every one of us. Send healing to the sick, to the bereaved and lonely. Also bless our pets that give so much love, and ask nothing in return.

Please Father God, allow our loved ones in spirit, and spirit guides to come close and be here for us, uplifting and giving us proof of life after death.

Amen.

A Poem

The touch of a hand

The wipe of a tear

A message from spirit

To say they are here

Reaching out to those in need

Offering relief to those who grieve

To touch a heart, to raise a smile

Bringing us uplift, once in a while

A message from God:

He knows you suffer so

He sends amongst us Angels

To help when we are low

Believe there's more to life than this

Our loved ones know its so

Sense their presence, feel their kiss

They're always here they won't let go

The Future

Many of our incessant questions concern the future. Where will happen next month, next year, in 2020? Will I be married or single, in or out of work, rich or poor, sick or well, living here or elsewhere, in this life or the next?

Worrying too much about the future can drive us crazy. On the other hand, a little bit of advance information can be very helpful. I have had the good fortune to provide many positive and accurate predictions for people. They are frequently kind enough let me know how things turned out for them, often months after our meeting, such as the lady who wrote the following letter:

'Hi Christina, Hope you're well! It's Lorraine. I don't know if you remember me, but you gave me two readings last year! Afterwards you gave me a lift back to Swalecliffe.

I just wanted to tell you, every bit of my reading has come true, and my life has changed so much in a year!

Thank you so much Christina

Take loads of care, loads of love,

Lorraine xxxxx'

Thank you Lorraine, for taking the time to write to me. Feedback like this does no end of good for a medium's reputation, as well being a tremendous personal boost of course.

People are very generous in their appreciation, not least those at the Open Arms Haven:

'For anyone thinking of booking Christina for their church or centre, can I say we thoroughly recommend her. She has worked for us several times at the Haven, most recently at our Christmas Special Night, and is a real favourite. She has the most amazing empathy and delivery – a real live wire on platform, but with the sensitivity to know when to bring it down a notch. She has delivered messages to me personally that were amazingly accurate – things no one could have known from someone who has passed only very recently – the lady has a real line to the Heavens, that's for sure! – Jay Gage'

This is high praise indeed. I hope I can continue to live up to it Jay.

I've been lucky enough now to work not only extensively around my home area of Kent and Essex, but with groups all over the country, including some wonderful people north of the border. At the risk of blowing my own trumpet too long and hard, this message records the success we shared in Scotland, as well as the efforts of my hosts, that helped to make it happen.

'Hello Christina,

A huge thanks for all your hard work coming up to Scotland to serve the four churches as you did. Ann and I were very proud to introduce you to them. Although we had not met, it was like meeting an old friend, and very comfortable to be with you.

All of the churches were delighted and would love to see you again. You brought joy and hope with the messages you gave, and to many, a comfort in knowing their loved ones were only a whisper away, and were still looking out for them as they did when they were here. To us, it was a joy watching the people in the congregation laughing, and very touching when they received the message they were looking for. You have been blessed with a very special gift. God bless you for the love you spread in the work you do. Hope to see you soon.

Take care

Ann and Arthur'

Ann and Arthur, through their hard work and warm hospitality to visitors like myself, are an absolutely vital part of the process of linking loved ones to spirit.

But let us get back to the subject of this chapter – back to the future. As I write this, I am busier than ever with private readings, platform events and other activities. Obviously I hope it carries on, and I can continue to use what capacities I have.

The fact is they seem to be getting stronger with time, and the thoughts and pictures I am now receiving from spirit are increasingly sharp, accurate and intense. Medium-ship can deal with the past, as in events that need to be laid to rest between spirits and their loved ones, and the future, as in the case of Lorraine's happy outcome.

What I did not appreciate early on was how the present can also show up in astonishing ways. Probably my most remarkable experience of this to date, took place in 2007. I was booked to appear at an afternoon of clairvoyance in an Age Concern Centre on the Isle of Sheppey. Present amongst the group was a lady helper, I suppose in her forties. We had just got going when I felt a strong pull towards this lady. I described a house to her in some detail. 'Yes,' she said, 'that's my house.'

I could see some kind of trouble going on outside the house, and asked her if there was any problem there at the moment.

'No,' she said, 'I've no idea what you mean.'

I said, 'I'm sorry to say this, but I can see a fight going on, right outside your house.' She didn't know what to make of it, and I turned to someone else in the group.

Half an hour later we were interrupted when some visitors arrived at the centre. It was the police, asking to speak with the lady I had been addressing. They told her, in front of everyone, that there had been an altercation outside her house, in which her son had been stabbed. This had apparently happened within the last half hour. As the lady rushed off, the group sat in stunned silence, me included.

I had never met this lady before, and knew nothing of her or her family. Neither had I seen her house or the road she lived in. From what the police had said, it seemed I had seen this event in real-time, as it occurred some distance away. I had never experienced anything like it before.

Spirit continues to light the way for me, opening doors, sometimes to reveal only further mysteries. Last year (2009) I dreamed again of the white building. There was the same black man in the white suit, the Indian temple, the judge and jury. As before the one in the middle spoke to me.

'Christina,' he said, 'you have completed seven life spans on the earth, this is your last time.'

I replied, 'Oh – then what happens to me after this life?' There was no answer.

So my future remains shrouded, on hold. By the time of my next book who knows, perhaps I'll have that answer and can tell it you – along with more dreams, more visions and certainly I hope, many more unique and uplifting experiences with people and their loved ones in spirit.

As for the future for clairvoyance, the paranormal has always been an area that's outside the mainstream, and we are unlikely to see school or university courses in the subject, though I hope people will increasingly explore and study it for themselves. I have the impression that we have but touched a snowflake on the tip of an iceberg in our knowledge of the spirit world. Who can tell how much more we may one day learn about the other side.

There have always been mediums working with spirit, and there always will be. As human beings we share a common experience – we are all born, and are as certain to die one day. As the Bible says, 'In the midst of life, we are in death.'

And what of your future? At whatever stage you are at in your earthly travels, always remember that this life is but a part of an infinitely greater journey of discovery. Those we love and lose along the way, remind us of the great mystery at the heart of human existence. The desire to know that one's family and friends endure, and the yearning to reach out to them, is in everyone. Someday, somehow, that will happen for all of us and there will be joy in our hearts, knowing that our loved ones really are only a breath away.

I would like to thank you for taking the time to read my book, and if we have not already met I hope one day we will. I wish you peace, goodwill, and harmony, in the knowledge of eternal life hereafter.

God Bless You,

Christina.